YOU'VE ALREADY WON

JOY R WASHINGTON

CONTENTS

Introduction v

Chapter 1   **The Beginning** 1

Chapter 2   **The Journey** 12

Chapter 3   **Discovery** 24

Chapter 4   **Evaluate** 29

Chapter 5   **The Unexpected** 41

Chapter 6   **Faith Comes by Hearing** 49

Chapter 7   **Perfect Love** 59

Chapter 8   **Trust in the lord** 72

Chapter 9   **Let's Us not be weary** 82

Chapter 10   **Detour** 91

Chapter 11   **Follow Me** 103

Chapter 12   **Expected End** 114

Chapter 13   **There is a Season** 122

INTRODUCTION

I KNOW THAT IT DOESN'T MAKE MUCH SENSE FOR ME TO SAY TO ANY of you that *"You've Already Won."* But you have, you just don't know it yet. The illness that has taken hold of you and won't let go. The war on your finances. The career that ended abruptly. The death of a loved one, and the marriage that ended in divorce. *"You've Already Won."* How? Because God has a solution to every problem. Whatever it is or was that you went through was solved long before your arrived on this planet.

The victory is never ours because victory belongs to God. Everything that happens in our lives good, and yes bad serves a greater purpose. Every solider must be battled tested, wounded, and made anew. In the journey of discovery is where we learn what our assignment is and who we are meant to be.

The problems that you inherited or were given, were not handed off for you to handle them. The struggle comes with batons. And whether you're sprinting, walking, or crawling, your troubles and your burdens are to be given to somebody greater, and someone who can in exchange "give you beauty for ashes."

Jesus said. "Come unto me, all ye that labor and are heavy laden, and I will give you rest. Take my yoke upon you and learn of me; for I am meek and lowly in heart: and ye shall find rest unto your souls. For my yoke is easy, and my burden is light."

Sometimes, the spiritual assignments that we have been given may not appear as "the gift" at all, but more so as a burden because of the complexity of the role we have been given. Life does not come with instructions. A divine duty does not come equipped with a GPS system with directions. What it does come with is prayer. A dialogue with God that allows us to "ask", seek, and to eventually find the answers and serve.

As we transform, we must get still. Getting quiet is a link to God's wisdom and his discernment. In other words, stillness is freedom. When you let go and let God, that is when things began to change. This is when the universe speaks to you and provides instructions that you didn't have in the beginning. As you align yourself with the powers of the universe, you will come to understand that the universe was already rigged in your favor. Ready to give you the life that you would have never expected.

The struggle is real. But so is the power that lies within you. Let's face it. Life is going to happen one way or the other. But it's how you respond in that moment that will determine how you view and understand the rest of your life. We have the power to change what we don't like in our lives. But for many of us it takes many mistakes, many lessons, and a stripping of the soul to discover like Dorothy in the "Wizard of OZ, we too always had the power to go home.

Until you recognize that the universe has anointed all of us with the power to overcome any hurdle, stumbling block, or challenge, that every situation that shows up in your life is given to you to teach lessons, strengthen your faith and layout the road map to your true destiny. *It is then that you will come to realize that nothing has the power to overtake you.* When you stop needing to have control over every part of your life, when you stop imitating God and take him out of the box that we are all guilty of placing him in, when you are tired, and have suffered enough, and you finally let go. There in that moment, is when you will know *"You Already Won."*

CHAPTER ONE

THE BEGINNING

I WAS 13 YEARS OLD, SITTING ALONE BY THE CAFETERIA WHEN I SAW the vision: A cloud in the sky in the shape of an open book, with a barely noticeable path just above it. The book cloud as I called it seemed to have captured my attention, and I stared at it for a while. I remember distinctly that it rained hard earlier that morning, so hard that the wheels on the school bus seemed as if they drove on top of the water rather than rolling through it.

It was a cold rain. The type of rain that was wicked and bone chilling, and it froze the tips of my fingers upon contact. I was no longer a pee greener, but a carrot top. I had somehow survived all the growing pains of a seventh grader and had blossomed into a curious, but quiet eight grader. I had come from the bathroom and suddenly I felt a nudge, a strong urge to make a left instead of my usual right.

The sun poked its head through the clouds, and I sat on a partially dry blue bench looking at the sky. All of a sudden, the landscape changed. I couldn't believe what I was seeing, and I couldn't take my eyes of it. Though I didn't know it then, God was speaking to me. The cloud that held my attention that day carried the shape of an open book. He knew I was curious, loved books, and would wonder what story it was telling?

1

At such a young age, I felt that the universe was communicating with me. It was odd how it caught my interest by showing me a book in the clouds that day. I know now what I didn't know then, is that God knows every like, every interest, and he knew that an open book in the clouds would stop me cold. He was right. In that moment, I had lost all track of time. All that mattered was the book that I was seeing in the clouds.

Curiosity had taken a strong hold on me. I just wanted a glimpse into the book. Since it had shown itself to me, a few words would quinch my thirst. To my surprise, the letters UCLA emerged, and my mouth dropped. From that moment on, I claimed UCLA and it would become the focal point of everything I did in my school life.

There was more to this story than the vision was willing to tell. I was determined to find out the part it wasn't divulging. Before my eyes the sun got brighter and the puffy white clouds that decorated the sky including the book cloud and the small path, vanished. I willed it to stay but like it had accomplished its mission, it left anyway. I had made that trip to the bathroom a thousand times.

I always Walked back the way I came without question. But that day was different. I felt a nudge, a slight push to take the opposite route and loop around the social science building. I had every intention of going back to class, but my travel was interrupted by something greater.

I still sat on the blue bench where parts of it were drier. The paddle that gave me permission to leave class and go the restroom, still lay in my hand. The quietness was departing, and the hyper voices of teens had grew louder in my ears. The next thing I knew, my best friend Joshua tapped me on the shoulder as the lunch bell sounded off. He could always feel things, and he could always tell when the truth was in me, but a lie came out instead.

"So, how come you didn't come back to class?" Joshua said with snicker in his voice.

"I…I wanted to try and beat the crowd and get our burritos earlier." I replied.

"Liar!" He said. "Something's going on, and I will find out what it is." He snickered again. "See, you didn't bring the paddle back." He looked at me strange. "Wanna go to Sevens?" He noticed the side gate was open.

Sevens was a discount store with a diner that we'd sneak over to and indulge in the three dollar fried chicken special, or for Joshua, the five dollar steak special both with mashed potatoes and gravy, a choice of mac and cheese, or mixed vegetables. I would always choose the mac and cheese, Joshua, it would depend. The gate was open, and to get by Mr. Parker, AKA, sharp eye, we'd buy a small combination burrito, and a small drink, sit at the corner table where the hyper kids, and chaos was taking place, and when he was pre-occupied, we'd race through the gate laughing.

By the time he figured out we were gone or thought we might have disappeared out of his watchful sight, we would be sitting under the huge Oak Tree eating cafeteria served lasagna with an extra side of French bread, and snicker doodles. The Styrofoam of the good stuff stayed in our backpacks tripled bag so the gravy wouldn't seep out. He'd stand by us, and we'd look up wanting to bust up laughing. But we couldn't. It was a dead giveaway.

"I don't get you love birds." He said, a smile in his voice. Mr. Parker swore on a stack of church bibles that Joshua and I were going to marry when we were old enough. So did a lot of people, but we knew better. We were sister and brother from different mothers, and I knew then and so did he that our relationship was unique as it was different. We both knew that the friendship we shared was bigger than the both of us. We looked at Mr. Parker and giggled at his remark.

"Oh, you giggle now, but I'll get the last laugh when I watch you walk down the aisle at the church."

"Not," we both said.

"Okay," he snickered. "Say," he said. "I appreciate you kids not taking advantage of me, or that gate being unlocked when Mrs. Vincent forgets to lock it after you kids leave. She's old. Worked here for 30 years, 10 years at Baker High School, and the old girl just forgets sometimes you know." He said.

We sat eating not saying a word just listening. I think Mr. Parker appreciated that. He was a talker who expected the young to listen and follow. He knew our parents. We belonged to the same church, and he lived just a block over. We weren't trying to be put on punishment because we got out of line with Mr. Parker.

"Well," he paused. Appearing to walk away, then pivoted and turned to face us. "You kids sure have some tough stomachs." He said. "When I saw you last you were eating burritos and drinking something or other. Now, you're eating lasagna and garlic bread, sugar cookies and milk. My." He shook his head. He tossed a hand and went back through the gate that we had escaped through to head to Sevens.

We finished the lasagna, French bread, snicker doodles and milk. Joshua as he always did, took our plates, and emptied them in the trash. The back door of the cafeteria opened, and it was a buddy of ours who lived in our hood, on the same street, a few houses down. Keisha peeked her head out of the door, looked both ways like she was driving. She beckoned us to come to the door and we did in a rush. Before Mr. Parker made his last round out front where our state flag flew high above the front of our school, Keisha took our chicken and steak platers and hid them in the frig.

To earn a box of big sticks, I'd get permission from Mr. Dakota my English teacher who was mesmerized by my love and knowledge of the classics in literature, and for that purpose he had no problem with me volunteering to wipe down tables in the cafeteria before our buses showed up. Mrs. Kramer had no problems with Joshua wiping down tables either since he was the only student who would challenge her to a debate in history class.

It got us big sticks, a big box of them. And we got to slip back to the frig and get the goods. The buses arrived in front of the school fifteen to twenty minutes early. Mrs. Crawford was always the first bus. She was a kind black woman who was a stickler for time and didn't take guff off the kids that rode her bus.

She greeted all us kids with a smile. Asked us how our day was, didn't allow open drinks on the bus unless it was water, or juice that was capped up in a bottle. Around Mrs. Crawford, all our names were either baby, sweetie, or suga plum. We used to giggle in the beginning of our journey with her, now we had gotten used to our pet names, which became our nicknames.

Joshua and I always sat together on the bus. We either sat in the front, Joshua's favorite spot, or somewhere in the middle where I liked to sit by the window, look up at the sky and dream. Today was my turn. We sat in the middle, and I sat by the window. Like teenagers, we giggled at things that weren't funny and didn't make sense.

Joshua and I were having one of those teenage moments with the giggles. My chuckling stopped the moment I connected with the blue sky and the fading clouds in the distance. Temporarily, I drowned out everything. The chatter, laughing, and even Mrs. Crawford's voice over the loudspeaker, telling us to buckle up and put our seatbelts on, was muffled. I searched for the book cloud like miner's searching for gold. Disappointed, I sighed, sat, and snapped my seatbelt in place and caught the look in Joshua's eyes.

"What!" I said sounding a bit snappy.

"Disappointed because you haven't seen lover boy, Picasso Brown get in his pops new Silverado." He grinned a smile I didn't like.

"I could care less about Picasso." I said. At the time I was serious. "I wasn't looking for him." I replied. "You'd never get it." I still looked for the book cloud. "Besides, his dad doesn't have a red Silverado, he's got a red Mercedes."

"See, you do like him." He grinned again.

"Shut up Josh." I said trying to hide my grin. Truth was, I liked Picasso Brown a lot. I got goosebumps just hearing his name. He sat in front of me in Algebra class and I found myself just staring at him especially when he wasn't looking. Mr. Phillips seemed to always call on me when my eyes were glued on Picasso and I looked like a deer in headlights crossing a busy highway.

As much as I liked Picasso and fantasized about him asking me out and asking me to go to the eight grade dance, in that moment he couldn't hold a candle to the book cloud that had my interest in a way that he never could. For the rest of my young life, I would look everywhere for the book cloud. After every rain, I'd rush outside and look for it like a skilled navigator. I would search each cloud, study every shape, even if that meant me getting Joshua to walk to the store to grab anything, just so I could get to a different area, hoping that new territory would allow me to find my book cloud. But it didn't.

For years I came up empty, but I kept looking. I had to. There was an open book with a tiny path behind it. Out of 989 students at King Junior High School, no one had seen it but me. I often wondered why it chose me, but I could never come up with an answer. So, it drove me to find out why? I had every intention to come back to class. But something happened that day.

The earth seemed to pause. The universe opened its mouth and spoke to me. There was an impulse, a whisper from creation that guided me from my usual route to a road less traveled. In a language all its own, it asked for me to sit, and I sat. I felt as if God had a long telescope pointed in my direction, and at the right time, he came looking for me.

At 13, my life had changed. Purpose had caught up with me, and I didn't know what had hit me. There was a story written in the clouds that intrigued me and I wanted badly to read it. For some reason, it hid its tale from me, and gave me only four letters from its thick book. Like a ghost, it haunted me. Like a page turning mystery novel, it kept me up a night.

My social studies teacher Mrs. Sal Lee had scheduled us time in the career center. She had talked about taking our class on an on campus field trip from the very first day of school. It was the new grandiose building that had started its construction of the career center at the end of the school year. Sometimes Josh and I would go out to the field, sit at the very top of the bleachers and listen to the sound of drills, and hammers, and watch the men take raw materials and construct walls that would eventually become a building that we would be able to go in.

That building was ready now. Mrs. Sal Lee was excited, a little too excited for me. Most of us were between the ages of 13 and 14. When we thought about careers, we looked to our parents, my father who made his bones in construction and who I was proud to say was one of the men beating nails in wood in the vacant lot across from our field, building our new career center.

Mama, looking back had the most important job. Managing eleven kids on a daily basis while daddy put on the hard hat and raced with the sun six days a week to pay the bills, buy us clothes, and put good food on the table. Mama had her own side hustle. She was a master at designing garments. I watched her take paper bags when she couldn't get to the fabric store to buy pattern paper for sewing to create her designs, turning bolts of material into flawless garments ready for the red carpet.

At 13, I was into books, having fun with Josh and, fantasizing about going out with Picasso. If this on-campus field trip got me out of Social Studies class, I was all for it. It's not that I disliked Social Studies, I just disapproved of the topics we were studying. Mrs. Sal Lee had introduced us to the ten themes of Social Studies. I was assigned to People, Places and Environment. Josh was assigned to Global Connections. I laughed so hard at his topic that I nearly peed in my pants.

Josh's facial expressions said all what his mouth couldn't. In all honesty mines wasn't all that better, but at least my topic, People, Places, and Environment would allow me wiggle room to explore who I was and investigate my own surroundings and the world around me. Josh was on the other side of the universe. At least that's how he felt.

One step outside of Social Studies class and his mood changed instantly. How could it not? As Mrs. Sal Lee unlocked the gate for all twenty-three of us to go through the entrance, the sight of fall greeted us. The trees that lined both sides of the field showed off their vibrant fall colors of auburn, orange, yellow, and bright red. The bold fall foliage on the trees was enough to say that fall had arrived. As the wind blew the hair off the trees, Josh tossed an armful up and the rest of us joined him.

It didn't take long for Mrs. Sal Lee to join us. Soon our poor field was decorated with leaves. To our surprise, our teacher Mrs. Sal Lee, tossed up a pile of leaves. it was easy to see the 13 year old crawl from her cellar and participate in the fun.

Once we stood before the steps of the career center. Mrs. Sal Lee had returned to teacher. We formed our usual two lines, girls on the right, boys on the left. She clapped her hands twice and like soldiers the chatter stopped, and we listened, already knowing what she was going to say.

"We are the very first class to see the inside of our new career center. Be on your best behavior at all times. I encourage you to ask questions as your essays depend on it." She said. "Now class, are we ready?" She asked.

"Yeah." We said, unenthusiastically.

"Really! Well come on. You can do better than that. Instead of a four page essay, I'll cut it down to three." She replied.

Life had come into our voices, and we sounded like a church choir on the first Sunday that had gotten the holy ghost. We rolled in the career center like tin soldiers uneager to discover what we would find. The center was huge, decked out in soothing colors of blues that automatically soothed my spirit and the temperament of our class. Before our eyes could adjust to the college size center, we were greeted and welcomed by a smiling thirty something lady with Lucille Ball red hair.

"Greetings, greetings." She said with an older lady smile. Of course, thirty something isn't old, but at 13, it was.

My eyes acted as camera's amazed at the layout. Cozy couches bursting of earth tone browns mixed with different shades of blues neatly fitted into the corner of the center. I connected to it immediately and had tuned out what the lady with the Lucille Ball hair was saying. My attention had migrated to the wall that showcased the big bold word "Discovery." Without thinking and without permission, I drifted from my peers to the comfy couches like some invisible force was guiding me.

Before I could sit down on the couch that looked like it waited for me to sit on it, was a college catalog stationed on the thick cinnamon wood table. When I saw the four letters on the catalog, UCLA, I didn't sit. I fell on the couch. Slowly the book cloud was revealing a tiny portion of its story. That day, it had only given me for letters. Today by some bizarre force, I was guided to the "Discovery area," merely to find the single four letters that the book cloud had chosen to give to me.

It wasn't long before Mrs. Sal Lee discovered that one of her ducklings had left the pond to journey elsewhere. By the time she had politely excused herself from the address, I had fallen in love and had given my heart to UCLA. The punishment she would choose to give me for breaking rank from the others and creating my own way, guiding my own tour, was soft to say the least. She expected a flawless essay, and to research more about UCLA since I was so interested in attending there.

She had taken a seat next to me and said nothing for a minute or so. She watched me get swallowed up by a huge University and fixated on the beautiful Royce Hall, that had a choke hold on my heart the way Picasso Brown never did. She allowed me to explore more through the catalog, and then she suddenly spoke.

"It's a great college." She said with a smile on her face. "Looks like you've found your topic."

"I'm going to college here." I blurted it out like I had already been admitted. Then I got all teenager again, "Am I in trouble? I…"

"Give me an "A" on the essay and we'll call it even." She replied.

I had missed the tour, but I didn't need it. In an odd way, something had gently guided me over to "Discovery," just like something had funneled me over to the lonely blue bench to see the book cloud, drop me four letters and direct me to the UCLA catalog that would began the transformation of my entire life. Though I was just 13, I seemed to understand that the tiny path that I saw in the clouds that day had reintroduced itself and allowed me to walk on its trail, even though I still didn't have a clue of where I was going, or what story would eventually unfold.

At a very young age, I was attracted to words. They had become my compass, my roadmap to a world that at 13, I was still trying to figure out, and determine where it was that I fit in. God had timed it all out perfectly. The rain. The urge to go to the little girl's room. My decision to turn left, and walk though the quad, rather than take a right and go back to social studies class.

God created a detour that I never even noticed. At 13, he needed to speak to me and send me a message in a way that I would receive it even if I didn't understand it. The four letters that the book revealed to me that day was a story: little by little the tale started to reveal clues, and like an inquisitive sleuth on a scavenger hunt, I was determined to read the mystery book in the clouds that had purposely exposed itself to me and uncover the tale it was keeping from me.

It seemed weird to me that I had been given four letters from the book cloud, and on an on-campus trip to our career center, I became immediately attracted to the word "discovery," and broke away from the group to find my way over to the section that introduced students to a plethora of college catalogs with life in them. As bizarre, was the UCLA college catalog comfortably sitting on a table and a couch waiting for me.

UCLA had come from the book cloud that was secretly denying

me its narrative giving me just enough to tease my curiosity, somehow knowing that I would want more. Little did it know that I wanted it all. But I had to play the books game. I had come to the conclusion enduring many sleepless nights that I had to accept that whatever minuscule clue the book was handing over, was to take it and run with it, and then wait for more as it chose to give it not as I wanted to have it.

It was a hard lesson to learn at 13, considering that perseverance seemed more suited for the older crowd. Books and the words in them had a powerful effect on me. The book cloud was no different. It wanted something from me, and I wanted to get something from it. Whatever the answer was, drove me. I never looked at the career center the same after that. My life had transformed on that damp, cold day in the quad when the book cloud introduced itself and changed my life forever.

CHAPTER TWO

THE JOURNEY

S OME OF US SPEND A LIFETIME TRAVELING ON DIFFERENT ROADS never quite getting to our destination. Why? Because we either didn't set a goal, or some old, defeated thoughts talked us out of pursuing what was already ours. We are not meant to be still or to get comfortable. **We are meant to move.** The objective is to get to your destination despite whatever obstacles may stand in your way.

Every human being owns this story. All of us at one time or another become intimidated by something that we determined was way out of our reach, so we didn't even try. **Dreams do not become reality by fear, but by faith and persistence. You cannot have a defeated mindset and expect successful results.**

What are you believing for? What is your spiritual GPS communicating to you? Are you listening to it, and more importantly do you have the courage to follow it even if it means that you have no clue of where you're going, and that you must become vulnerable to a power that is greater than yourself. You see a Part of the journey is self-discovery. Who are you and who were you meant to be? What did you come to this planet to do? And what is your authentic assignment?

The purpose of the journey is to get still and listen. This may mean that you have to turn off life for a moment and get away from your job, your kids, your studies, from a routine that has blocked your communication with the universe and tune into a frequency that's different, that aligns with your spirit and speaks to you in a way that you have not been spoken to before.

Are you really meant to be that hedge fund manager? Or are you meant to teach kitchen table economics to poor families who could use your expertise in budgeting and learn how to invest a few dollars a month to help them dig their way out of poverty and live the life that they were meant to live. Are you a person whose never had a stable place to live, but you have it in your heart to build a city for the most vulnerable who suffer the same plight as you? Who are you? And what is your spiritual assignment?

Our real assignments show up, or present themselves when we least expect it, or when we are just not ready for distractions to make themselves present in our lives. My best friend Joshua Rollin was not immune to this occurrence. Joshua, God bless his soul came from a family of dysfunction. There was no physical abuse, but his mother was a drinker and loved to to entertain friends with music, partying, and sometimes food.

Nadine Rollin loved her Jim Beam, loud talking, and gathering with her crew like a fish to water. After five on Friday's, it was on. Her porch went from being still to the meeting place, where us kids saw a portion of adulthood come to life.

Mr. Rollin was never home when Nadine communed with her drinking buddies. He was a military vet that had his bright mind stripped away from him by the cruel life of service, and never got it back. These were the times where his nerves were so bad that Nadine would have to hospitalize him and ease him away from life into an environment that offered him some sense of comfort. Prayers, therapy, and medication would always bring him back home.

Usually, when Mr. Rollin made his way back home. He'd do good for a long while, and out of the blue something would tip him off and

Nadine would have to take him back. It was a lot on Joshua's family and ours. Our two families were one big family that just happened to live in two separate houses.

Joshua wore his father's illness, and his mother drinking and partying with a smile. But his eyes were a window, and through them I could see his soul and how he really felt. His pain was deep. His sorrows an understatement of how it made him feel. He was rapidly pulling off the clothes of a boy and jumping into the cloak of a man without guidance from a father whose illness prevented him from helping a teenager grow into a man.

Without knowing what he was fully doing, Josh gravitated to the old G's in the neighborhood running errands for them, moving heavy boxes with the men as they shucked and jived about the women over-stuffing items they'd purchased and never used, and hid in corners of their garages waiting to be moved. Josh was average height, handsome, and thin. To look at him was to assume that he couldn't lift a cracker Jack box, let alone a woman stuffed container. But Josh was stronger than even he gave himself credit for.

He got pats on the back from men who rallied around his pops, offered him smokes while they chugged down a beer, talked about family, and fixing things, and how good of a young man Josh was turning out to be. That's when I kept my distance and let Josh marinade his mind, and spirit in manhood. That's when I watched from my parent's bedroom window a crowded porch of older men guiding him and preparing him for a life that I couldn't.

The end of the school year was approaching, and Josh and I were graduating from carrot tops to become freshmen at Malcom High School come fall. We both had an older sister at Malcom already. Mines a senior, his a junior. Malcolm was a tradition in our hood. Everybody went there except for the rowdy ones that just hung out and got into trouble.

We weren't allowed to hang with them. If we got curious there were serious consequences. Josh and I had seen enough of those consequences with our older siblings. Being the youngest had its privileges, and we had learned how to get in the kind of trouble where it earned us more chores, a dollar taken from our allowance, or a weekend without riding our bikes to pick whatever fruit was in season, which sucked.

There was a barbeque planned for the weekend for Josh and me. We were held in high esteem because we had gotten promoted to the next level in life, and for our parents and elders, young adulthood was forthcoming. We were drawn to the back by the smell of daddy's barbeque ribs. Josh and I raced to the backyard trying to beat each other into the gate, knowing that we both couldn't fit at the same time.

He caved and showed he was a gentleman and let me enter first. The men watched and laughed. The women grinned and shook their heads, some whispering about us joining hands in Marriage as early as after high school. Their match making made us laugh and we tuned them out like we tuned out Mr. Iverson's dog Scout barking over the fence, hoping for a piece of barbeque to fall.

There were tables of food set up nicely by the orange tree in our backyard. We helped ourselves to some hot barbecue ribs and chicken hot off the grill, drenched in daddy's own barbeque sauce. I opted for the chef salad over the potato salad. Josh of course helped himself to the potato salad, filling up his bowl. I licked out my tongue and said "Yuck." He laughed and placed a spoonful in his mouth.

I grabbed us drinks. A crème soda for Josh and an orange soda for me. He added sweet white corn on the cobb that was serenaded in butter. I grabbed us a helping of mac and cheese, and sides of greens and cornbread.

As I ate, I watched the story unfold. Mr. Rollin sat with the men, a smoke in one hand, a beer in the other. My eyes raised out of my sockets as I was surprised to see Mr. Rollin drink a beer. He was a quiet, thoughtful man who felt at home with the men folk and talked with them like his mind wasn't sick. I hadn't a clue of what they talked about, but I saw him toss his head back in laughter and raise his soft voice over the men like daddy who was loud.

I had caught a long draw of his smile and then switched my eyes to Josh, and there it was, Mr. Rollin's smile plastered on his. Nadine had always said that out of all of her son's, Josh had caught the bug of her husband Booker. I didn't pay what she said attention at first, but now I did. Josh was every spit of Booker, and now it was becoming more plain why he hurt the way he did when he had to go away.

I was full and couldn't eat another morsel. Josh went back for seconds, and I often wondered where he put all that food in such a lanky frame? He burped loud and laughed. I laughed to, then smacked him on his thigh. It was all surreal for us. Come fall we were going to be freshmen. New school, new people, football games, dances, proms, homecoming, and the spark in our souls that made us dangle between young adults and adults.

Beyond graduation, we had graduated into something bigger than we knew. The adults could see it and we could feel it. While Josh and I indulged in conversation, and made our own predictions about who of our peers would hang around until graduation, who would drop out? Who'd get pregnant, and who would become a star? Mr. Rollin was rolling out the rectangular shaped cake.

An older brother of mines whistled to get our attention. To our surprise there was a beautifully decorated chocolate cake with two green graduation caps on the cake and cream cheese frosting acting as our tassels. The cake was too beautiful to cut, but before I could refrain, Josh cut a slug, then cut it again and placed the extra large slice in my plate. Laughter and claps roared from our backyard, and I nudge him in the side.

Life was never dull with Josh, which is why I chose to hang out with him verses his bossy, overbearing sister who was just two years older than us. She didn't get me, nor I her. But Josh did. We had gotten each other since our pre-school days, and it had been like that for us ever since. Mr. Rollin stood and walked over towards Josh and I and handed his son a small box that was gift wrapped in shinny silver wrapping paper with a beautiful silver bow.

Josh paused from eating his chocolate fudge cake and smiled at his dad. He shook it, then opened it, and found a stunning Timex watch inside. His expression said all what his mouth filled with cake could not.

"Every grown man needs a watch son." Mr. Rollin said, as he snapped it on Joshua's wrist. Joshua hugged his pop like he didn't want to let him go. They embraced like I had never seen. Soon the backyard erupted in cheers and claps. Like the girl I was, I broke out in tears like Nadine, Mama, and the other women.

Josh turned to me and wrapped an arm around me and pulled me into him where my head lay on his shoulder. He knew my tears well and he understood why they had fallen. They were long overdue, and we both knew it. Mr. Rollin was like a father to me, and it hurt me to see him go back and forth to the VA hospital as much as it hurt Josh.

Neither of us looked towards the wedding planners that had us saying our own vows before we could talk. Instead, I turned and hugged Mr. Rollin after he presented me with a crisp one hundred dollar bill, then hugged Daddy as he handed me a mid-sized Journal with a lock and key attached. It was my favorite color, a Christmas blue. On the top left corner of the journal was a cloud in the form of an open book, and the inscription below read. *"Life is a journey, keep searching."* I nearly dropped my journal. Josh had quick hands and caught it like he was recovering a fumble.

The look in his eyes spelled trouble for me and I knew that the moment we had some Josh and Meka time, I'd be bombarded with questions that I didn't want to answer, but that he would persist until I did. Like Christmas and birthdays jammed together, we were both graced with more gifts then I'm sure we deserved. I received a kindled, Josh a 23 piece kitchen utensil set for barbequing, an initiation into the men's club.

He raised his set high in the air like a proud 14 year old and received a chuckle from the men who had stood in his shoes. They treated him different than they did the other older boys on the block. He had gained their trust like the other boys didn't. He borrowed their tools to fix things. He cut each one of their lawns, so they didn't have to do it.

He sat with them on warm summer evenings, talked and jived with them. Though he didn't know it, he had gained their wisdom. They could see it. But for now, he couldn't. He was blinded by the dizziness of his youth. He was still a yearning soul, finding his way, and so was I.

The weekend had come and gone and so had our graduation party that had come with it. To wake up on a Monday and not have school was heaven. In my mind, I had my whole day planned, and I was eager to get to it. I brushed my teeth and washed my face quick and showered even quicker. I smelled the aroma of morning coming from Mama's kitchen. Somehow it smelled a little sweeter.

The scent of bacon, mixed in with Johnny Cakes, and hot buttered maple syrup was almost too much to bear. I envied the older adults who had put in the work and had deserved a breakfast like this on a Monday. I yearned for the days where I could sit out on my lanai and have a breakfast like the one Mama was serving. Today would be that day for me. The dining room table and the view of our front porch from our dining room window would have to do.

Like clockwork, Josh announced himself. He kissed Mama's cheek, sat, and served himself a helping of Johnny Cakes, and bacon. It appeared that we were both in a foot race with each other to eat, and in a sense we were. He poured us both a glass of milk. I drenched my Johnny Cakes in hot maple syrup that Mama had made. He followed, and our stomachs were grateful for it.

We cleaned the breakfast dishes swept the floors, wiped down the counters, and dried the dishes and put everything away for Mama. The least we could do for a Monday breakfast like that. Mama smiled, and through her eyes, we could see surprise and that she had checked off a chore from her list. She hugged us both tight, kissed our foreheads, and thanked us, then asked.

"What are you kids gonna get into today?" She asked sitting at the dinning room table, lighting up a smoke.

"To the bookstore first," Josh said. "Meka wants to look at some new books, and I want to comb through some of the new magazines."

"Well, good for y'all." She made circular rings with her smoke. "Always good to be learning something." She drew another puff. "What else?" She took her last puff, then put the cigarette butt out. "Cause I know that you kids ain't trying to stay at no bookstore all day no matter how much my daughter loves books."

We looked at each other and giggled like teenagers without answers do. Really, all we were looking to do over the summer was to grow and find out answers to questions that burned deeply into our souls. The book cloud still boggled my mind and stirred my soul for answers to a story that was stingy and sent me on a wild goose chase of discovery. And now, my father of all people had bought me a journal with an open book, shaped like the one I had seen that day in the clouds. Even it had a message.

Josh had stumbled into this horrible query encounter. His had started way before we stepped into the career center. Mines lite fire the day that I did. Nadine, God bless her soul did the best she knew how with six children and a husband who found reality in another world that was safe for him. He didn't have a pop to play ball with. A pop to show him how to tie a tie, or how to be a man. Or help him inquire about what he should do with the rest of his life?

He had two older brothers, and two older sisters, one two years older them him. What advice could she give to a boy who needed a dad to teach him how to become a man? Everette, and Chase had went to Malcolm back in the day when both of us were just snotty nose kids running around the gym like the every ready bunny's kid's on a mission.

They both played basketball with my brother Jared and collected a championship trophy for their team.

They had girlfriends and little brothers just got in the way of what they knew as men. So, Josh was left to fend for himself. That's where the old G's came in, and that's who Josh drifted to when the boy in him needed lessons on becoming a man. How we hooked up was genius. The universe and the stars looked for something different and somehow Josh and I showed up.

Across from the farmer's market was a park. As kids, we went to Vision Park a lot. Weekends Daddy made it a point to take all of us kids to Vision and let us play until we nearly dropped. When Mr. Rollin was feeling well, he'd always tag him to come along, and he would gladly. Mr. Rollin would join daddy in swinging Josh and me on the swing. Booker got a kick out of hearing us scream. His laughter and his smile showed it. It was a huge park with an Olympic size pool, basketball and tennis courts, a massive field to play all sort of games, soccer, baseball, and football.

Today, as we bagged fruits and vegetables for Mr. Ward's customers at the farmer's market, something snapped inside of him. His eyes locked onto the tennis courts as he watched two guys play. Since I had known Josh, I had never seen him that engrossed in anything accept feeding his stomach.

"Be right back." He signaled to Mr. Ward, and me, I guess.

"Where are you going?" I asked. As if I didn't know. He didn't say a word. He just pointed to the courts and started walking faster as if he had the next game to play.

"Ah, let him go." Mr. Ward tossed a hand with a smile. "Besides you, the young man sees something that he's interested in." He looked up from bailing the boxes. "He's a good kid, and so are you. Don't worry." He said. "I doubt very seriously that even that could take him away from such a pretty filly like you." He giggled.

"It's not like that Mr. Ward." I replied. "Josh is like a brother to me.

We're just friends, and it just so happens that we have a lot in common. I don't know how so many people get that wrong? I assure you nobody would be saying it if he was a girl or if I was a boy." I said. "I guess we just mess people up because we're opposite. It doesn't get us though." I said as I helped him bail.

"Of course, you don't get it honey because you're young now, and I suppose he doesn't either. But give it a year or so, and things will be turning around. I promise you that." He wiped his brow. "Besides," he said. "You got nine brothers, why in the world would you want or need another one for?"

"It's seven Mr. Ward, seven." I laughed. "I know you don't get it. But Josh really is my brother. I learn a lot from him, and he learns a lot from me. Is that so weird?"

"The learning no. The friendship yes." He reached into the storage closet, got the broom, and started sweeping. I took the broom from him and continued sweeping, by that time Joshua had returned.

"Find what you were looking for?" Mr. Ward asked.

"Maybe?" He hunched his shoulders. "The guys said that they teach free lessons here every Thursday. I guess it wouldn't hurt to come and learn?"

"Nothing beats a failure but a try." Mr. Ward said.

Joshed looked at me as if he were seeking conformation. "What are you looking at me for." I said. "Go for it." He grinned and poked me in the side. I poked him back and Mr. Ward got one of those adult smiles on his face like Josh and I were about to go fool around or something.

We burst out laughing as we finished cleaning for him. We had become immune to that sort of talk and all the weird looks that had come with it. Yeah, they were the adults, but they knew absolutely nothing when it came to me and Joshua. Happy, married adults were always looking for the next young love to blossom and in some way shape or form, fall prey to the love that had goosed them in the behind.

Unfortunately, they were looking in the wrong place when it came to me and Joshua.

Our payment for helping Mr. Ward was bringing home as many fresh fruits and vegetables as we could carry. I loaded up on the Washington delicious apples, and the pink ladies for me. I wasn't really an apple fan, but my family was. It was one of Mama's requirements that we eat them to keep away certain cancers and to keep our bowels lubricated. She was a southern who had reached way back in her family history. Since it had worked for them, she had deemed that it would work for us.

None of us questioned it, not even Daddy. But why would he, he was a southerner too. Josh was a lover of plums, and peaches. His bag nearly ran over with them. For Nadine he'd bring Brussel sprouts, broccoli, and cauliflower. For Mama, rice, and beans. Daddy grew everything else. In fact, lots of what Mr. Ward sold came from Daddy's garden. How he managed to plant and harvest our huge garden working twelve to fourteen hours a day stomped me. But he was a farm boy who brought the farm out to the city.

I stopped at the door and paused before I got on my bike. Josh turned his Huffy Mountain bike towards Mr. Ward like he knew what I was going to ask. I'm sure he did. Before, I could get the question out of my throat, Mr. Ward grinned, chuckled, and said, "You two can start tomorrow. Hell, you're here every day just about. Besides, this young man is going to be taking tennis lessons across the street on Thursday's." He cleared his throat. "Seems like it's in the good lord's will. I'll pay you at the end of next week." He said.

We put the bags in our baskets and jetted out of there. It didn't even occur to us to ask him how much he was going to pay us. Mr. Ward was good people and the one thing he didn't know how to do was sell people short. The burning sun had cooled, and the summer air was thick and neutral. Restlessness had struck me, and I wandered out to the backyard.

To my surprise, daddy had came through with his promise and put a Hammock out on the sturdy Oak trees that illuminated our backyard with peace. I rushed to it and stretched out in it. Immediately I felt a sense of Comfort that seemed to escape me inside of the house. Since I couldn't seem to find the book cloud anywhere in God's sky, I decided to stare at it on my journal that Daddy had bought me and try to read more of its story.

My eyes had moved from the book cloud on the journal to the bold caption written beneath it. ***Part of the journey is to keep searching.***" A weird feeling came over me, and in a strange sense I felt like the universe was speaking to me again. I felt like something was egging me on to start journaling. In the left hand corner was another inscription that spoke to me and solicited the question that at 14, I was still trying to figure out. There was something out there in our backyard that day. Whatever it was it had waited patiently for that moment to speak to me and tease my curious mind. It didn't hold back asking me the question that I had begun to ask myself after I had seen the book cloud. ***"Who are you?"***

CHAPTER THREE
DISCOVERY

A T SOME POINT OR OTHER, ALL OF US ARE IN SEARCH OF OUR purpose, who we were meant to be? Why did we come to this planet? What's our unique assignment? It must be more to it than showing up for a job that you hate, or have outgrown, or living a life that doesn't quite feel like it's yours anymore. So, what is it, what on earth were you meant to do?

For starters, we were meant to listen. There is a still voice inside of all of us that speaks consistently and never shuts off. It is our spiritual GPS that comes equipped with directions, routes to get you through the detours, warnings of life traps, and every divine tool needed to get you where God has always intended for you to be. The trick is to tune in and listen.

Have you ever been guided to do something outside of your realm? And the whisper was so strong that no matter how you resisted, you had to act on it. Did you take a walk, but this time you took a different street, and in so doing you ran into an old friend who reminded you of your dream and wondered if you pursued it?

The hammock became my sanctuary and Josh's to. After work at the farmer's market, we'd hop off our bikes, race into my backyard and hop onto the hammock and just get still. In my stillness, I got a chance to get a peek inside of my own life that I didn't know exist. It was as if life waited for me on the hammock and as serenity prepared me it spoke.

The book cloud had given me four letters: UCLA. Through a random trip at the career center, those four letters breathed life into a college catalog that guided me over to a cozy corner with a couch that intentionally waited for me. I treated the college catalog like a novel, combing through every page. Each word spoke to a piece of my future. Each sentence expressed development, and each new chapter I explored granted maturity.

Though the book cloud had hid itself somewhere in the vast blue sky, it had transformed and communicated to me through the feisty winds that had commanded attention on a warm summer day. By its own accord, it chose Joshua's Sports Illustrated Magazine as its vehicle of engagement. I watched in amusement at first while Josh tried to hold his pages down in frustration. Besides his dad, and the men who spent time grooming him into manhood. Authur Ashe had become his new hero.

As the pages of his magazine shuffled almost rhythmically, I saw the word **unlimited,** and for some crazy reason I wrote it down. Then came the word **courageous,** not knowing why, I wrote that down. I was focused now on the dancing pages and like I waited for another word to present itself and it did, came the word **light**. As I laughed behind Josh's frown, the final clue revealed itself this time in the form of a sentence, rather than just a single word. It was an advertisement with a lady sitting on a yoga mat, hands folded, legs perfectly straight, eyes closed, and hands placed together as if she were praying. Somehow my eyes caught it before Joshua turned the page. *"Aligned with a power greater than yourself."*

Without warning, the winds stopped. What was left of their display was gentle, trickling winds that bent the heat and barely made my bangs move. Now, it had engulf my curiosity again. I read my chicken scratch that I scribbled down and at first it made no sense, then the light came on. Those scribbles defined the power that God had given me for the rest of my life. It was bigger than the four letters I had been given that day. Through some old feisty winds, God redefined what UCLA symbolized for me. Each letter was a symbol of who I already was and why I was given the assignment in the first place.

The book had begun to reveal the story that I wanted so badly to read. In Being quiet, I had come to understand that letters were turning into sentences. Somehow the four letters that I had seen during my carrot top days in junior high school were bigger than I could ever imagine.

Stillness at any age makes you go deep inside and take inventory of where you are in the moment. It, (quietness), forces you to get honest with yourself and have an open dialogue with God about purpose. Because, let's be honest, at some point in our lives we want to know why God even bothered to bring us to this planet. Stillness is God's way of letting you tap into the question that plague's many people for years. All we have to do is stop talking, shut out noise and just listen. The answer will come.

When the answer does show up, the question then becomes are we brave enough to follow the path? At this point it can become scary, following a route that you're unfamiliar with, and not accustomed to taking can paralyze your thinking and stop you from moving forward. Once you focus on the enemy's greatest weapon, *"fear"*, you change the trajectory of your power. Fear replaces truth and suddenly, there is a change in direction, which eventually leads to displacement and disappointment.

This is a classic example of how blessings are delayed, but never denied. ***A mismanaged step in your road may inflict you with challenges and obstacles. But it will not stop your blessings.*** Stumbling blocks and trials only come to make you stronger.

The teeny path that had made itself known to me in the clouds began to align itself within my heart. In the beginning the way the Book cloud presented itself to me was all I thought about day and night. The miniature path that stood sharply behind the book cloud earned a few glimpses but nothing more. The more I journaled and the more I lay focused in the hammock, *"my burning bush"*, I felt as though God was revealing small pieces of my purpose that he knew I could handle.

I could gobble up a novel like a hungry man feasting on a good cut of meat. Words pinned to a page in a book allowed me to travel the world I was sure that a little black girl from the Eastside would never see. I was introduced to customs, cultures in foreign countries, and movements in this country that kicked down the doors of oppression and built new bridges to freedom.

Books had given me hope in a world that wasn't always kind to girls or boys who looked like Josh or me. Writing had offered me freedom, a space, and a voice I never knew that I had. I felt boundless, vulnerable, and unlimited. Something had changed in me though I hadn't identified what it was. Josh had changed too.

He had grown a few more inches, and his slender arms formed muscle, his Chest was slowly taking the shape from boy to man. His skinny legs looked as if someone had gently blew air into them and left a tight bubble on the back of his calves. His voice had gotten deeper, and his laughter heartier, and courageous. In a few short lessons, he was becoming a heck of a tennis player.

My appetite had increased and now I was writing about everything. Life had become a story for me. The slightest thing peeked my curiosity and before I could think, words were flowing from my brain like water finding a route in the vast ocean. I wrote about things that I didn't know that were inside of me like crazy stuff, like how the book cloud was some sort of divine sign by God giving me a small look inside of my future.

How could I help it? That day had haunted me since the day it happened. There were nearly a thousand kids at my junior high school, and out of all of the kids at the school that day, it chose me. To date, I hadn't told anyone about what happened. I was too afraid of what people might think. I knew what I saw, and I didn't want anyone telling me what I did or didn't see.

I hadn't told my mother, hadn't told my father, and the big one, I hadn't told Joshua. I could tell Mama anything, Daddy most things that didn't include boys. Joshua, well, what hadn't I told him? Part of it was that I didn't know how to explain it. The other part was that I was still trying to make sense of it, so how could I make it make sense to them? All I knew at this point was that I was following some sort of path. Why? I was still in search of? When Josh and I got on out bikes and took to a trail, it was strictly for the love of fun and adventure. Whatever fun or adventure we stumbled upon, we made the most of it, and at the end of our escapade, we'd find a healthy Oak Tree, or a big Sycamore Tree, plot underneath it and teenage.

The universe had opened up and taken me into a new world in which I felt unready. I was a kid processing adult language that was oh so foreign to me and I was figuring it out as I went along. I was overwhelmed at times and in those times, I wished I wouldn't have seen the book cloud at all, or the tiny path behind it. I was about to be a freshman with the world in front of me. New people, cheerleaders with attitudes, jocks who swore every girl wanted them, even the geek girls.

I was scared. Not about going to high school, but about this new life that seemed to be placed upon me. I didn't feel that I was equipped, but something bigger than me did. I was growing out of my body at a pace I couldn't control. And there was a fire inside of me that I couldn't put out, nor cool.

Lots of questions loomed inside of my brain and I contemplated many things. I was given a blank sheet of paper by the universe and told to write my own story. I struggled much at times. But what I didn't know was that at the age of fourteen I had already won.

C H A P T E R   F O U R

EVALUATE

T̲HE LAST WEEK OF S̲UMMER WAS HOT, AND DRY. T̲HE WIND IF there was any seemed stingy and pre-occupied, making it a chore to lay in my hammock and receive guidance from something so immense that it blew my mind every time I thought about it. It knew me, and it seemed to have an insight on my future, and it wanted me to follow a fixed route to get there. That much I knew.

For years, I thought only adults got the call. Obviously, I was wrong. At fourteen, I didn't know God had a long telescope that was equipped to look in on anyone, wiggle a finger and dispense his angels to bring the message. God did not have respect of persons, but I had to learn that.

Age was just a number to God, and it seemed that human beings made a bigger deal out of it than the universe ever did. At the tender age of twelve, Jesus dialogued with the elders of the church and fascinated them by his wisdom and knowledge of a world in which he had only been a part of for twelve years. At the ripe age of 88, Elizabeth brought John the Baptist into the world, and at the seasoned age of 90, Sarah gave birth to Isaac, when according to science, both were well pass childbearing age. Consider Moses, born at a time when the Pharaoh of Egypt declared that all Israelite babies be killed. By God's fate Moses escaped death and was brought up in the Pharoah's palace, and later in life, God commissioned Moses to deliver his people from enslavement.

God wiped out the age thing as he had definitively given me an entire range of people in which he had shaken a finger at and not only did there lives change, but by there mere existence, they were afforded the power to change the world. This made me wonder if I would change the planet and have an effect on humankind? At 14, my story was barely being written, my purpose in the infancy stages where I was still in discovery, detecting things about me that had just agreed to come to surface.

I was lathered with questions like a wet bar of soap. I was taken down a path I didn't ask for nor did I know. But I followed because the book cloud would not allow me to rest until I found the answer and acted upon it.

Maturity wise, Josh and I were a head of our freshmen class and some of our sophomores. The book cloud had changed my trajectory. The path that he had introduced in the clouds that day, led me to the hammock, and Josh to during warm summer days and spoke to us. High School was a training for real adulthood. It was a road map to either success or failure, and the choices you made determined it all; do overs, a slippery tight rope, depending on your slip up.

Day one, I saw the poplar jocks, cheerleaders, and their flock in the center of the quad drawing attention to themselves through noise, food fights, immature chasing, and through sheer stupidity, bull dozing themselves into the spaces of the smart kids, the nerds, geeks, or whatever they were called back then just because they thought they could. It sickened me every time I saw it, and I found myself defending them because one, I couldn't shut my mouth.

"Hey," I said. "Leave them alone and stay in your lane."

"Why don't you mind your own business freshmen?" One of the football jocks said.

"Make me." My smart mouth shot back.

Josh stood and tossed his tennis racket around, never taking his eyes off him.

"What freshmen, you're gonna hit me with that thing?" He stood and came closer.

"If you want it?" Josh turned his body fully towards him. "Come get it."

He took his dare and charged toward Joshua. My eyes widened as I had never seen Josh like this. Before he got to Josh, my older sister September stepped in front of him, a look of displeasure covering her face.

"Really Moose." She said, frowning as she handed me a chocolate milk and chocolate chip cookies, and Josh a plain milk with snicker doodles.

"Sett," he said, eyes large and wide like he had just seen a ghost. "Hey," his frown turned into a smile. "These your folks? I didn't know. This one must be your sister, looks just like you."

"Yeah," she looked at me. "My baby sister with the big mouth. Her apology name is Meka, and her bodyguard here is "Joshua." She looked at him in the same way she had looked at me like the moment Moose turned his back, we were about to get cussed out.

"Nah," he tossed a hand. "It's cool. Gotta make your mark coming in here, right?"

Moose and my sister were friends if you could call it that. She tutored Moose and had gotten his academia up to speed to play the game that he loved. For that, Sett was a complete angel in his book and could do no wrong. Sett could never stay made at me long. For an hour or so, I was in the doghouse, but by lunch she and her friend were taking Josh and me to lunch off campus. Big deal for a freshman.

In the weeks to come, I learned a lot about Moose. Outside of football, his life was tough. His mother was very ill. His father worked two jobs, and Moose worked part-time at Beets Market to help his family though his dad didn't want him to. Behind the façade of being tough,

Moose was a kind soul. I had gotten to know that side of him because I had learned to shut my mouth long enough to listen.

It was the Saturday before Halloween, and Mr. Ward sent Josh and me to Seth Farms to purchase fresh corn, a mix of white and yellow. You could see the corn fields for miles. When the wind swept across the corn fields and tickled the stocks it spooked us in a fun way, and we'd jump off our bikes and, run through the corn. We'd yell and scream like Jason was chasing us with an axe in his hand. Nearly every time we'd run into or come close to running into Seth, we'd get spooked all over again.

For the life of me, I don't know what made us do it. Fun and being young, I guess? It was like the wind played hooky in life for a brief moment, and the second it saw Josh and I hop off our bikes, it would strike. Seth did what he always did, laugh, and point us in the direction of the white and yellow corn, allowing Josh and I to pick ours fresh like Mr. Ward liked it.

Josh ran down one side and me the other. That's where I ran into Moose and screamed. Moose screamed too and nearly dropped his bucket of corn. Moose was six feet six, 280 pounds of pure muscle. Whatever work out Coach Avery had him doing worked out with his body. He laughed after the fright and took the bucket of corn and placed it on his right shoulder.

"You scared the crap out of me." He said.

"Well, you scared me too." I replied. "I wasn't expecting to see anyone."

"Ditto." He said.

"You don't strike me as the type of guy that scares easy." I added.

"On the whole I don't, but I got a lot on my mind." He said.

I paused, sat my bucket down and looked at him, and he at me. He wanted to talk, and I wanted to listen. But instead, he lifted the bucket of corn back on his shoulder, however something stronger took the bucket from his shoulders and forced him to vomit life from his mouth.

He looked at me again and began picking my corn as if he knew what he was doing. As he picked, he talked. I followed and listened.

Mooses' real mother was an alcoholic. She drunk up until the day he was born like her life, or the life of her unborn child didn't matter. Moose was taken from his mother when he was just a month old and adopted immediately by the Gentry's. Bizarre, the Gentry's baby died weeks earlier from crib death. Moose had seen pictures of his brother who died and according to Moose, the two babies bore a scary resemblance. It was as if God took the sick one and replaced it with the healthy one.

Two years after Moose, his adopted mother gave birth to two twin boys. Briefly Moose had stopped picking my corn, and a smile glided across his attractive lips. His eyes sparkled as he spoke about his twin brothers, and he laughed hardy when he shared a memory of them passing water from their diaper on his favorite pair of pants and laughed.

Moose smiled as he dug the memory from a special place from his past. "Life was actually great then." He said as he went back to picking my corn. "Then all of a sudden," he shook his head. "Hell broke loose. Just like that my mom got sick, and life just hasn't been the same." He finished picking my corn and sat the bucket down. "If my mom doesn't get a heart soon, she's gonna die." He looked me dead in the eyes, and I broke down and cried.

Moose pulled me into his arms and held me there. Too much was going through my young mind at that moment. At 14, all I could do was cry. It was the only way I knew how to handle it. In a month's time and some change, the adult world had leaped into my space, and I hated it. I wasn't ready, at least I thought I wasn't. If this was the rite of passage to adulthood, I wanted no part of it.

Moose wiped my tears with his soft hands. He placed his cheek on the top of my head and rubbed my back. I knew I had to do something, but I didn't know what. Moose and I had bonded in a way that I would have never expected. From that day on, our relationship was never the same.

The seven minute bike ride to Mr. Ward's farmers market might as well had been seven hours. I couldn't get Moose off my mind. Josh had rode way ahead trying to force a race that normally I would have accepted, caught him, sometimes passed him, and sometimes losing to him by a hair, only to hear him brag about it for a week. He stopped and waited for me. By the look in his eyes, I could tell he knew something was wrong. He turned to me and just starred like he was reading pages from a juicy book.

"Did Moose do something to you?" He asked. His eyebrows narrowed. Pre-age lines strolled across his forehead that were premature and were decades away from taking their rightful place.

"No, Josh. His mother is gonna die soon if she doesn't get a heart." I said. "Come on."

"Wait," his eyes widened. "You mean Moose, big old defensive end six foot six, 280 pound Moose?"

"I don't know of another one." I replied getting on my bike. "I gotta do something."

"Wow!" He said, getting on his bike. "What can I do to help?"

At that moment, I felt as if the universe was hearing my heart. Joshua wasn't a fan of Moose nor Moose of him. Neither of them had gotten over there man cave brawl. The fact that Sett had interfered with their dual had only heightened their dislike for each other. Maybe it was the way I said it? Maybe Josh's heart was softening and something bigger was taking place?

Honestly, I didn't know what it was. But I knew Josh better than anyone except for his mother Nadine. Something had gotten in on the inside of his heart and chiseled away at his nemesis that he willfully carried towards Moose. On his own, Josh would have never wanted to help Moose with anything.

We dropped off the fresh corn to Mr. Ward and left. The ride home was as quiet as a stone resting in a stream. I parked my bike outside of our backyard gate. Josh parked his.

To our surprise, Mama was laying in the hammock that had become our burning bush. She rose as we approached and welcomed me with a big hug, then Josh. The hug she gave was like a holy fire anointing my soul.

"Come here," she said. "Come sit and tell Mama what's on your heart, cause I know something's wrong. My heart has been on you all day."

Mama was part Cherokee and she had been given the gift to sense fortune as well as tragedy. She could see auras. Once she saw through our television screen Nadine's entire family except for Booker die in a tragic car accident on their way to the Carolina's to visit family for summer. I remember Mama hopping up, leaving her house shoes in front of the couch, and darting over to Nadine's to try and halt the trip.

I remember the look in Nadine's eyes. She looked like she had been run over by a freight train and struck by lightening all at the same time. In that very moment, the world seemed to have gone silent. I could see Mama's lips moving, but her sound was muted. So was Nadine's. Nadine's body language said it all.

First, she stumbled backward with her hand across her chest. Then, her suitcases tumbled one after the other as if they were an assembly, falling out of her car each sliding in their own direction. Promptly, there was a rushing of all six of her kids including Joshua out of the car. The red Hawaiian print dress detailed her nervous heart palpating at thousand beats per minute.

While Daddy and my brother's sat the table for diner, it was Nadine who rushed over beating at the front door like something bad was happening. Daddy looked up and paused putting down the plate. "Come on in Nadine." He said. "Is Booker alright?"

"Booker be fine." She said.

At that point, Mama had stepped in the living room, changing from her cooking clothes to her dining garb. A blue shift accented with red sleeves, and a red ruffle that hugged her just at the tip of her knees. Her right eyebrow stood up, and her look concerned.

"Did you see the news?" Nadine said. "Did you see what happened to that family going to Disney World in Florida?"

"No." Daddy said, arms folded across his chest.

"No." Mama followed shortly behind him. "What happened?" Mama continued. "You looked as if you've seen a ghost."

"A family of seven, six children, and a mother died in a car crash heading across the state to Florida."

Both my parents looked at each other. Daddy knew all to well about Mama's gift. He called the boys over and us and we all joined hands in prayer as Daddy prayed for the family that had gone and praised God for the one, he had spared. After that day, the entire community recognized Mama's gift. Nadine made sure of it.

Her instinct was at work again, I could see it. Josh could see it to. I took a long deep breath. Before I could get Moose out of my mouth, she turned to me and said. "Moose and his family will be just fine. His Mama is gonna be around here a long time, and she is gonna see that young man do some great things. This is just a test."

I fell into her arms and just cried. Mama didn't even know Moose. And it wasn't like he ever stepped foot on our property. Moose was as foreign to Mama as snow in the desert.

The look in Joshua's eyes made me laugh. It was a mix between being spooked and like what the hell. Because of Josh, my fowl mood had changed. Suddenly I had an appetite. I'm sure Mama sense that too. Why else would she have oversized croissants that she made sandwiches with sitting on the patio waiting for us?

Josh grinned sheepishly then looked at the hammock as if it had some sort of cryptic message. It didn't. That was all God, pinching off a piece of his long telescope and giving Mama the nod. I couldn't blame

Josh. Sometimes I didn't understand it. I needed to laugh, and he was good for me in those moments.

Mama walked away, headed back into the house to put the finishing touches on dinner I suppose. I stopped her as she was about to go in the back door.

"What can we do to help Moose?"

"Pray for his spirit and pray for direction." She said.

"How do we do that?" I asked.

"Just say lord help, be open, and God will do the rest." She replied, blew a kiss, and entered the back door.

It was her idea to place Moose's mother Olivia on their churches prayer and visitation list. It was Josh's idea to start a go fund me page for the family expenses. Mama, Nadine, and their mission sister had organized "meals to heal." A group of church folk and anyone who just wanted to help make meals for Moose and his family every day. Also a group of us teens created rotating schedules to clean, do laundry, cut grass, and run errands.

Like dominoes, boulders begin to fall off Moose's family's shoulders. Mr. Gentry no longer needed to work two jobs to support his family. Through the help of the church and our community, Mr. Gentry, Moose, and his twin boys turned an old tool shed into a warehouse and revisited an old family heirloom, making custom made furniture. They started with a few customers wanting a chair, a rocker, and old couch upholstered and restored to new. Like a wildfire, the Gentry's had struck a chord and Mooses' father Noah had to hire new employees to keep up with the orders.

I had gotten the opportunity to meet Olivia on a Sunday evening after washing dishes. She didn't look like anything that the image in my mind had formed. Her green eyes had so much hope in them, and her smile lit up a room. It was easy to see where Moose had gotten his from.

The support had done her spirit good. Her appetite had much improved. For dinner she asked for seconds, enjoying Mama's pot roast, gravy and biscuits. I washed down the kitchen counters, and the dining room table. Josh swept the kitchen floors and emptied the trash. As I dried the dinning room table, I caught the last two minutes of 60 minutes.

Dr. Edward Davis was a heart surgeon who had a track record of operating on patients that most heart surgeons wouldn't give a penny for their lives. He hadn't lost a patient. He was extremely expensive, and he wasn't the type of surgeon to where you could walk into just any old hospital and ask to speak to him. He was like a high profile agent that only took referrals from a bourgeoise clientele.

I knew he was the one the moment I laid eyes on him, and I knew I had to find someway to get to him and convince him to operate on Olivia. As we entered the living room about to leave for the evening, Olivia took hold of my hand and held it for a minute. "You're one special girl." She squeezed my hand gently. "Thank you for giving my family hope, and my Moose life again."

"We all pitched in and just wanted to help." I said.

"You're daughter is something else." Olivia added. "I know she makes you proud."

"She does." Mama lit up like a sunshine at night. "She's a good kid most of the time." She kissed my forehead. "Moose and your twins are special too." She smiled when she looked at them. "The future is bright for them, and it's even brighter for you. Prayer changes things." Mama said. "Never forget that." She pecked Olivia on the cheek.

Olivia squeezed my hand tighter like she didn't want to let it go. She looked at me for a minute then said. "You should come over some time and visit Moose."

I was stunned by her bluntness and suddenly I was lost for words. So, was Moose. When I did find them, or when they decided to come from my mouth, I said something off beat and embarrassing now that I think back.

"I don't think Jazmine would like that." I replied.

"I don't think Jazmine has a choice." She shot back. "Besides, my Moose can't seem to keep you out of his mouth."

For me, the room went dark. I knew that everyone's eye was on Moose and me. I don't know whose mouth dropped to the floor first, Mooses' or mines. The look in his eyes said his mother wasn't supposed to tell his secret. The look in mines said I just wanted to get the hell out of there.

Josh teased me for days. When I saw Moose, I avoided him like the plague. That was until I got the news that his mother had a turn for the worse and was in the hospital fighting for her life. I couldn't sleep a wink, and in my restlessness, I put my heart to a letter and certified it the next morning to Dr. Edward Davis. The chances of him answering me was about as promising as me hitting the Powerball twice.

Before school, I went to our church, kneeled before the alter and poured out my soul to God and just cried. I asked for some sign of hope that Olivia would live, and then Josh blew into the church like a whirlwind. I wasn't in the mood for jokes, but it seemed that in the moment God had a sense of humor. Josh didn't say much. He just grabbed me by the arm and practically threw me on my bike.

It was an easy ride from the church to Hope Hospital. Josh nearly picked me up off my bike, locked our bikes quickly, and rushed me into the entrance. The lobby was full. The moment I saw Mama and Daddy, I got scared. Daddy should have been at work by now. Poor Moose weighted heavy on my heart and now I felt guilty for avoiding him.

Mama and Daddy walked over to where I was. Immediately I asked them if Olivia had died. There was silence and I broke down and sobbed miserably. Daddy wrapped his arms around me as I wept profusely.

"I sure hope those are happy tears." A voice I didn't recognize said.

"What?" I lifted my face from Daddy's chest.

"I'm Dr. Edward Davis." He said, extending his hand. "You must be Meka, and the author of this letter."

"I…yes." I was absolutely stunned. "But I just certified the letter this morning." I wiped tears from my cheeks.

"Something bigger than us is at stake here. You're letter moved me and touched the core of my soul. After reading it, I knew I had to come here, and I had to meet you." He said. "You're quite the wordsmith. That's some young lady you got there." He spoke directly to my parents. They smiled proud and grinned like treasure cats. "I want you to know that Olivia is in good hands and she's going to be fine."

"Thank you." I said, tearing up.

"No, thank you."

CHAPTER FIVE

THE UNEXPECTED

"We know that all things work together for the good of those who love God to them that are called according to his purpose." Romans 8:28

WHAT DOES THIS ALL MEAN? HOW DOES IT RELATE TO YOUR experience? It means that God's plan will not be put off. That, no matter how your situation looks. No matter how impossible it may seem? How much your doctor is telling you to get your house in order. How bad your finances are, the fact that you lost your job and that you're about to be evicted. God is in control. He sees the big picture. He holds the future and the *"Great I AM"* has the master plan.

Most of us are programmed to focus on the problem not the solution. Maybe we think that if we consume ourselves with the problem long enough that we will be able to solve it. Whatever you're going through right now. Whatever is keeping you awake at night is not meant for you to solve. As a matter of fact, it is not meant for you to be bogged down with it at all.

I think as humans we confuse our duties with God's duties. Our job in crisis is to *"be still and know that he is God."* Believers know that through the power of faith as small as a mustard seed, can get God's attention to grant change immediately. Do you worry about the chair you sit in clasping each time you sit in it? Do you wake up in the middle of the night worrying if in the morning you'll be able to hear? Do you worry about being able to see when you've been privileged to see the earth with all its beauty and wonders all the days of your life?

No, you don't. We expect that each day we will see, hear, and not find ourselves on the floor by the mere fact of sitting in a chair. Is this not faith? "All" means everything, even the burdens that we cannot carry. The sudden storm that just dropped in your lap. The unexpected firing at a company you've worked for 20 years. The sudden relationship with a person that you were determined to hate. *"All things."* All of it works to his advantage, to his good and most important, to his glory. ***Nothing is coincidence. Everything that happens serves a purpose.***

Nearly two months into the school year, I had a run in with Moose. The smoke screen that he allowed me to see was not who he was at all. He had fooled me miserably and like the teenager I was then, I reacted off sheer emotions and so did he, and so did Josh. What I didn't know was that even that moment served as part of God's plan.

Even after our run-in, I hated Moose. I owned his fake story more than he did. The Moose I was introduced to was a bully who thought it cute to prey on what he assumed to be weak brainiacs because they used their minds and he his size, which at best gave off a false bravado. In all honesty, Moose didn't except himself. Without warning, he wandered into a space, an arena where the unexcepted was the norm for smart kids, and the butt of jokes their springboard to success.

They knew they weren't accepted. Moose didn't. His skills on the football field and the wannabe's who followed him, and Jazmine, the varsity cheerleader who worshipped him should have been enough. But it wasn't. Truth be told, Moose wanted to be one of them and thought he could never be one of them, so he targeted them for who he was not. I hated him for it until I was graced with his authenticity. Though I fought it, I had to change towards him.

I often wondered how my sister had the audacity to tutor such an arrogant, and cocky being. Sett had a temperament second to Jesus Christ. I asked her once and she laughed and looked at me strange. The way older sister's look at little sister's when they say something dumb.

"He needed my help. So, I helped him." She looked at me and shook her head.

"Just like that," I replied.

"Yeah, like that." She smiled at me and then plucked my thigh. "He needs football. I think it frees him."

My look was even stranger than hers. Maybe he did need football, but how would she know that it freed him? She was starting to sound like Mama. But of course, Sett had the gift of sixth sense too.

What I had come to learn was that it was divine purpose. All of it. Even the run in at Seth's Farms was a part of it. Josh and I had been to Seth's Farm a gazillion times and not once had Moose popped up. But on that weekend before Halloween, there he was planted on the same corn fields as me. Little did I know that my life would forever change, and so would Mooses'.

It was meant for Sett to tutor Moose, and for us to have that confrontation in the way that we did. It was also destine that we met sporadically in the cornfields and for Moose to divulge his story. Mooses' mother needed what he didn't have, a heart. What was left of his had transformed into a rigid stone. It wasn't because he was a bad person. It was because he thought she was leaving him. For that, he was blue mad, and it dictated everything that he did.

To date, the open book that lent its spirit to the cloud that day was revealing the story that I so much wanted to read. At the time I saw it, I was crazy curious about the story within it. Because I had an insane love for books, it drew me to it like a fish to water, and like a magnet to a piece of metal. What I didn't understand then, was that the story had to be written first and it wasn't. Life had to open for me and for words to hit each page, and I had to meet Moose for that to take place.

The immature hatred that I adopted towards Moose vanished. In the moment he exposed his story, I couldn't even remember the animosity that I once had for him. Earlier on, I wanted the worse for him. Now, all I wanted to do was help him. The universe opened itself unto me because I lost the ego, became unguarded and asked for it. Unexpectedly, it responded and offered me Dr. Edward Davis, the top heart surgeon in the country. Without hesitation, I took it.

Before Olivia's surgery took place, her body needed to align with her spirit. Her body had grown tired. Her heart slow and weak. Mama claimed that her body was flirting with death and old man demise was pushing her spirit away from her because he wanted her. Mama stated that Olivia's spirit man had spoken to her and that it needed help with positioning itself so that they could join together and welcome healing.

The community that rallied around Olivia and the Gentry's was the same faith unit that started prayer visuals at the church, and kneeled by her bedside with praise and supplication, sending request to God for healing. All at once, Olivia began to eat. Little by little her puny appetite increased. Her thirst for water intensified, and within days she was eating full meals. Through the power of persistent prayer, the spirit had positioned itself inside her body and death escaped on his carriage alone.

I returned to what drew me and what had spoken to me. The hammock awaited my body, and I awaited its wisdom. It had changed me. Groomed me for the cause and pushed me to a purpose bigger than myself. It had sat out a table and anointed my soul for a greater cause. It prepared me for the grueling task of helping Olivia, and giving me a courage I didn't know I had.

via Olivia, I walked through the shadows of death. And through people that I may never had gotten to know, he brought comfort and peace, and help. I was never without support, and certainly not alone. I came to understand that for this purpose I was chosen, and that the universe had my back.

At exactly 9:11pm, a shooting star blasted across the sky as if it were in a hurry. At 9:15pm, I received a call from Moose that Olivia would be receiving a new heart. At 11:11pm, Olivia was carted off into surgery. By the time I woke up and had breakfast, Mama informed me that Olivia was in recovery in ICU. from Josh I learned that her doner was a 20 year old female name Faith who unexpectedly died in her sleep of natural causes. Josh claimed that when the hospital retrieved her body that she had a smile on her face.

I wouldn't have believed it but the surgeon who removed her heart took a pic of the young woman who died suddenly. He was taken it by it, and according to Josh was stunned by the smile on the deceased woman's face. It was said that the surgeon described the smile as unusual and as if the woman had left this earth doing a great deed. He received permission from the deceased woman's family to hand over the picture to the family getting her heart. According to Josh, Moose wanted me to see it. So, he showed it to me, and I nearly fainted. Josh caught me before I hit the ground. Suddenly the prayer that I prayed came before me.

In an awkward way, I felt her spirit. She was the shooting star that darted across my path, flying like she was on a mission, like she was in celebration, and she was. She communicated to me that she had been offered a deal that she could not pass up. Eternal life in exchange for leaving her heart to Olivia and that was scheduled to put on her immortality clothes. There were things that she hadn't accomplished and a family that still needed her. Olivia was free to have her heart. Where she was going, she didn't need it anyway.

Moose couldn't be pried away from the hospital. Coach Avery, God bless his heart understood. Coach Avery knew that Moose was the goat, and to miss a practice here and there was no big deal. His game never lacked, and his dominance on the field was why Coach gave him lead way, especially since it concerned his mom.

The moose I first met was gone. I couldn't remember him being that way and it was weird. What was bizarre was that Moose and Josh bonded. It was hard to imagine two adversaries, now friends. They would sit in the quad at first break, laugh and talk like they had known each other for years.

They talked in between classes, at second break, and if I didn't drag Josh away for lunch, he and his new pal would yap through our entire lunch and beyond about boy stuff, I guess? They were the new odd couple, and I didn't know if I should be happy for them, or envious. At some point, I knew that Josh would find a guy friend that he could talk about things that he couldn't dare talk about with me. He probably assumed that I would discover a gal pal for the same reason he did. I just never expected it to be Moose.

There were so many lessons to be learned here. The first one I had learned was never assume anything. I thought high school was going to be parties, proms, football games, and boys. My first year was none of that.

I went to football games sure. The homecoming dance was just a few weeks away. With all what was going on, I hadn't even thought about attending. As a matter of fact, I didn't know if I wanted to attend. In helping Olivia, Moose, and the Gentry family, something shifted in me, and I wanted something more than what I had come there for.

Olivia had moved to a regular room in Hope Hospital. She was eating everything but hospital food. Meals to heal brought her breakfast, lunch, and dinner. Along with bringing meals, they sat, visit, gossiped, and played cards. Olivia was new, and her new heart seemed as if it were a perfect fit.

Dr. Edwards claimed he had never seen a heart that fit into a chest cavity so easy and so well. He professed that it felt as if the heart was guiding him rather than he guiding it. The letter I had written him had gotten passed up all the way to the Chief of Staff who couldn't believe a kid had penned a correspondence to get such a high caliber heart surgeon like Dr. Davis's attention. Adults saw it as a big deal, but I didn't. In my opinion, it's what any human being would have done.

Olivia could have been my mom, anybody's mom for that matter. In my gut, I felt compelled to do something. Olivia deserved a chance at a new life, and her family deserved to have many more years with her. I had gotten to know Dr. Davis well. He couldn't seem to get the letter I wrote on behalf of Olivia out of his mind. In fact, he confided to me that my letter changed the way he thought about medicine and the world of science as a whole.

I couldn't explain it. Didn't know if I ever could. Something hit me cold in the cornfields at Seth Farms. It was almost as if God performed heart surgery on me regarding Moose. It was as if our hearts spoke the same language. Played the same cord and beat the same beat.

He possessed a determination I had not seen. A friend of his was a big wig at one of the top papers in the country, the Banner Gazette. Mamma received the call first. She was excited as a quarterback avoiding a sack and tossing a hail Mary for a touchdown. She nearly pulled me into the front door as I arrived home from work, smelling like citrus and pinecone.

"It's him. It's Mr. Dyson the Editor and Chief of the Gazette, and he's calling for you." She was beside herself.

I was a dear in headlights, eyes as clueless as a cat caught in mischief.

"Say hello baby. Say hello to the man for God's sake." She said, still beaming with excitement.

"Mr. Dyson." I said. Surprised I could remember his name.

"You must be Meka." He said, a smile came through his voice.

"I am." I replied.

"How are you?" He asked.

"I'm good. Thank you for asking. How are you?" I said.

"At my age darling, you roll with the punches and forget about complaining." He laughed. "I guess you're wondering why I'm calling?"

"Yeah," I said. "I would guess that you don't make calls like this every day."

"You would be right." He said. "But I don't get phone calls from good friends of mines by the name of Eddie Davis about a young lady with an incredible gift to write."

I paused. Mouth wide open, eyes bulged out like I had been frightened by something. My Heart rattling inside my chest. "He…"

"He did." He finished my sentence. "And I can see why. This letter was not just a gift to Olivia, but to the world of literature. Meka, you are blessed with a special gift, and I'd like to offer you a column of your very own to continue to inspire the world by your words."

"Me," I said. Me…are you serious?"

"Can't think of a time that I've been more," he said. "It's a column I've been waiting to do for years, but I hadn't found the right author until you." He replied. "The column is called hope. Think you can bring us some great "hope" inspired stories? Do you think you'd be interested?" He asked.

I had taken Mama's persona, yelling and screaming in insane excitement, saying yes long before my mouth did. Mama took one hop and landed into our kitchen. I don't know how I managed to get out the words as nervous as I was, but somehow, I did. She said yes, then I said yes. The drumbeat in my heart intensified.

"I don't know how to thank you Mr. Dyson." I said. Excitement still looming in my voice.

"You just did." He replied.

"Can I ask you something?" I asked.

"Sure, Shoot." He added.

"How do you know Dr. Davis?" I asked.

"Eddie and I met in college in our freshmen year at UCLA."

My eyes bucked out, and I dropped the phone.

C H A P T E R   S I X

FAITH COMES BY HEARING

"So, then faith cometh by hearing, and
hearing by the word of God."

Aт some point, life will make you listen to it. The mes- sages are often gentle as an innocent breeze. With most of us, it goes unnoticed for days, weeks, maybe even years. Out of the blue life hits, and we wonder why we didn't get a sign and God wonders why you weren't paying attention.

To many of us, the world can be a noisy place. From the morning alarm clock, the dripping of fresh brewed coffee, the sound of breakfast, kids, spouses and traffic can drown out God's voice. Thus, God's message can get lost in a big pile of void. How do you hear above the noise? And how do you know when God is speaking to you?

Call it instinct. Call it something grabbing hold of your attention that stops you cold, and the feeling that comes over you is something that shakes you, baffles you, and no matter how you toss it off your shoulder it keeps hopping back on. Call it the universe opening the entire sky, and landing in your ear just to whisper at first.

With me, the hearing was a nudge, a sense of direction to choose to double around the quad before heading back to social studies class. The murmur teased my ear when the message showed up in the sky in the form of a cloud shaped like an open book. What I know now that I didn't know then was that hearing is trusting what God has spoken. At 13, all I knew was that I was seeing a cloud in the sky in the form of an open book. The more I stared at it the more it revealed itself.

Eventually, the book revealed to me four letters, and a tiny path that resembled a road. The road in the cloud in time sent our entire class to the career center where I was introduce to a college catalog with the letters of UCLA on it. Later, I became acquainted with Moose, and through Moose I learned of his mother's debilitating heart condition. The Message hit stronger this time and I was motivated to act. In acting to help Olivia, seeing a two minute interview on 60 minutes, I was introduced to a premier heart surgeon, Dr. Davis, and without a doubt, I knew I had to write a letter to him on Olivia's behalf.

At the end of the week Olivia had returned home. Her welcome home party had been delayed for a couple of weeks or so. Neighbors trickled in from mid-morning to early evening to cook, visit, and sit with Olivia. Moose was beside himself. A new Moose had burst from dying roots of a complex young Man who was scared of a future without his mother in it.

Jazmine, the head varsity cheerleader, took full advantage of the situation. She was determined to be Mooses' girl no matter what it took. She made herself overly available to cater to Olivia's every need. If the men folk were talking and laughing about it, then it was a big deal. Daddy, and his crew made themselves invisible to what they called women stuff. But they found a way to talk about Jazmine trying to get at Moose.

I was privileged to be a part of their wolfpack, and that they trusted me with their secret. I never said a word never even mentioned that I had caught all of them red handed eating up Jazmine like she was a seasoned piece of catfish with a side of hush puppies. My laughing and my turning of their mouthwatering Barbecue said they were safe. And when they saw it, their Dominoe tournament continued.

Olivia was vocal about Jazmine. She confided in the women that sat with her that she didn't trust her motives. That who she was really catering to was her son Moose, and that she was just an instrument to get her to him. I laughed at Olivia's truth as I wiped down her kitchen table and put the leftovers away.

Olivia's eyes watched me like a good driver paid attention to traffic. Her look was focused, telling, and with a plan. Olivia was taking short walks now. Noah was passed excited and looked forward to taking hold of his girl's hand and walking with her a short distance to the park. I cried the first time I saw them walk together, and Josh the brother that he was, let me have my moment on his shoulder.

He didn't say very much at all. Mostly, he just wrapped an armed around me and let me cry. Nadine watched from her front room, a huge smile looming from her red lips. She had planned Joshua's and my wedding the moment we leap out of their wombs. She didn't need to go searching for a daughter-in-law, she already had one. In time, Nadine felt Joshua and I would see that too. We didn't. But we could never convince Nadine of that, so we quit trying.

Josh was too excited about my new column. Before I could tell him not to, he spread it around the school like a wildfire hunting dry brush. Principal O'Neal went nuts and announced it over the loudspeaker at school during first period, and I just about crawled under the desk. Days later and to my surprise, there was a special assembly honoring my accomplishment. This time I couldn't hide. Josh was on one side of me, and Moose on the other.

Principal O'Neal acted like a preacher and hammered home the importance of caring and stepping up as a human being. I knew nothing about who he was. I wasn't a kid that was going to be getting in trouble and building that sort of rapport with him. I was too afraid of Mama showing up at school waiting in the principal's office with a look of annoyance in her eyes. Also, I didn't want daddy to come home from work and take a seat on the side of my bed and clear his throat. We all knew what the clearing of the throat meant.

Principal O'Neal was not letting me escape without saying something. This was the part that I disliked, and the part that I wanted to sneak away from. But I couldn't. I took a deep breath looked at Principal O'Neal, Moose, and then Josh, and took my place behind the podium. I took another deep breath and decided to say something. I went pass the column and went straight to Olivia.

"I don't know what got into me." I said behind the rustling of laughter. "I wish I could explain it, but I can't. I couldn't see Moose, nor his family without a mom no more than I could see myself without mines. Some things in life we are just called to do." I said. "I couldn't have done any of it without any of you." Tears surfaced in my eyes. "I wrote the letter to Dr. Davis because in all truthfulness, I was desperate." I replied as laughter ensued. "But I had a mustard seed of hope. I had no idea that a letter to save a life would grant me favor, and award me a column. I didn't do it for that. All I can say about all of this is that "All things work together for the good, to them that love God, to them that are called according to his purpose."

Moose wrapped his strong arms around me and held me, with his cheek nearly plastered to mines. I felt his lips close to my ear, and then his voice whisper softly in my ear. "I love you Me. I love you."

I went blank at that point. I don't know why I just did. I was still getting used to the new Moose and the old Moose was still peeling off my exterior. Principal O'Neal wrapped his arms around me and told me how proud of me he was, that he wanted to meet with me and my parents next week about a project that he wanted me to be a part of. He smiled. I smiled and then Joshua and I embraced.

"I could smack you. You know I don't like this kind of stuff." I said.

"Yeah, so, "He replied. "You needed to come out of hiding. Olivia would have never received that transplant if it weren't for you." He looked at me the way he looked at me when he knew that he was right. "You're a leader and you have to start acting like it."

I suppose I looked at Josh like I had lost my mind. For a moment, I did. As long as I had known Josh, he had never said anything like that to me. I knew he meant it by the look that stood bold in his eyes. I was too shocked to say anything, so I did what I always did in those moments, I just kept quiet.

I felt a strong hand on my lower back rubbing it as if I needed it. I turned and it was Moose. He smiled and gave me a look that I hadn't seen from him, and a look that no girl ready for a boyfriend wanted to see. Out of sheer nervousness, I looked towards the middle deck of the seats in the gym, and my eyes seemed to find the eyes of Jazmine that locked into mines and cut into them like a twelve inch sword.

I looked at her and smiled trying to convey a message that she destroyed long before it got to her. Mooses' hand was study, his rub even more studier.

"Mom wanted to know if you were free for dinner tonight." He asked. "Just so you know, she said she's not taking no for an answer. I swear to God." He grinned.

"Ah…" Josh interrupted my speech.

"We'll be there." He replied. "Hey Jazmine." He said

"Hey." She said, ignoring me, rolling her eyes.

"Catch you later man." Josh smacked hands with Moose.

"For sure bro." Moose smacked hands with Josh, his eyes planted on me.

I grabbed Josh's arm and nearly pulled him out of the gym. He looked clueless as if he hadn't an inkling of what was going on. Away from the gym, in front of the little theater, I stared at him like I was mad and wanted to fight. I wouldn't physically fight Josh. In fact, Josh and I had never even had an argument. Mentally, I was whopping his butt. He knew damn well what he was doing, and it was pissing me off that he was trying to be so darn sneaky about it.

Moose was attractive and it was easy to see why the girls at school went bat crap crazy over him. He had a body that could make the fast girls try and whisk him in a hidden corner, and good girls fantasize about naughty stuff they shouldn't. His indigenous blood was heavy. Raven colored hair, high strong cheek bones, and the strength of the God's in his smile. His black blood showed up in his herculean body, his savvy, and his sneakers. At any case, he was a junior and at our high school anyway there was a rule that forbad upper-class men to go hunting in baby fields.

In my opinion, Moose was caught up into the moment of all of us working so hard to help save Olivia. If Jazmine would have done the same thing, he would have never known that I existed. School let out early on Friday's. Malcolm had been doing minimum days since my older brother's attended there. Us kids didn't questioned it. We just counted down the time and when the bell rang, it was a stampede.

Josh and I didn't work on Friday's, but we stopped by the Farmer's Market anyway and helped Mr. Ward the same as our scheduled days to come in. He'd shoo us out, but until we had bailed boxes, sorted, and stacked veggies and fruit, and swept for him we wouldn't leave. He'd shake his head, and toss a hand, and go back to the back to make himself and us a sandwich.

"Me, Josh, come on back here and get you a sandwich." He'd say. "Maybe this will get you crazy kids out of my hair." He laughed. "Don't you and your boyfriend have something to do?"

"Now we do." Josh bit a plug out of his sandwich and chugged down some ice cold milk.

"Well good." He said. "Mighty proud of you Me, and Josh for doing what you did, and getting all of us involved to help Olivia get better." He took a bite of his sandwich. "With you young folks, the world's gonna be in good shape." He said and took another bite. "Heard you got a column in the Gazette." He replied. "Ooh," he whistled. "You gotta get up pretty early in the morning to get the Gazette's attention." He looked at me and smiled proud. "I know your folks is proud. Hell, we all proud." He took more bites of his sandwich and drank a glass of fresh squeezed apple juice behind it.

"Thanks." I said.

"That's what I've been trying to tell her. Me is too modest sometimes." Josh smiled and finished his sandwich and milk.

"Maybe?" Mr. Ward smiled. "She's young. You're young. You'll both grow into the clothes of life that don't fit you now."

Josh and I looked at each other and laughed. We were clueless to what Mr. Ward meant. Elders could say the darndest things sometimes and expect the young to just get what they were saying. We didn't most of the time. The laughter that churned out of our gut was just growing pains. Like what else were we supposed to do?

Josh and I had finally arrived home. Mama and Nadine didn't like for our bikes to just be laying out in the driveway or laying crazy by the fence. We liked the thrilled of hoping off our bikes and racing across the grass into his house or mines whichever we felt. He raced into his house changed his clothes and hurried back over to mines like it was important. At that age, everything was important, especially hiding secrets from your parents.

He waited for me in our Hammock. I ducked under the sack and took a lay right next to Josh with my journal in my hand. Josh turned to me, and I could tell by the way he was looking that he had something to tell me. He hesitated like he knew he had to tell me, but he needed to figure out how to do it.

"Just say it." I put down my journal.

"That obvious," he laughed.

"Yep." I looked at him. "Pretty much."

"What do you write in that thing?" He asked.

"About the book cloud I saw in the sky at King that day." I said, just blurting it out surprising myself.

"About what?" His look was weird, and he sat straight up.

"A cloud in the shape of an open book in the sky, and a tiny path above it." I said looking at him like I was sitting atop of the quad across from the cafeteria again.

"You saw a cloud in the form of an open book, and a path behind it?" He said, looking like he didn't believe me at first. "When? And how come you're just now telling me about it?"

"Because I thought you wouldn't believe me." I said. "It was October 20, and I will never forget. I had to go to the restroom. Instead of going back the way I came, I took a left and sat for some reason and boom, there it was." I replied. "It was as if something guided me to take a left rather than a right."

Josh turned towards me and in his eyes, I could see that he believed me, and that he wanted to know more. "What!" He sat up. "What did you do?"

"I was shocked at what I was seeing at first." I said. "So shocked, that I just stared at it, and in my complete daze, I lost all track of time." I replied. "Wanna know something really weird?" I asked him.

"What? What?" He was curious.

"I saw four letters inside of the book." I said.

"For real," his voice got heightened. He quieted himself as he looked all around as if someone had heard him. "Are you serious?"

"Yes," I said. "As a heart attack."

"What were the four letters?" He asked.

"What were you gonna tell me?" I flipped on him.

"You are not playing with me right now." He said.

"Yeah, I am." I was a smart aleck about it. I even licked my tongue out at him. "Spill and I give."

"Me." He looked at me. "I hate it when you do this." He sighed and looked at me like he wanted to toss me off the hammock.

"Promise you won't say anything." He said.

"Like who am I gonna tell," I replied.

"Me, damn you." He said. It's Moose…"

"Moose, what?" I suddenly rose up. "What's the matter with Moose?"

"Nothing, accept he's in love with you." He said with such conviction in his eyes. "He's got it bad. He's gonna marry you watch. I kid you not."

My mouth opened and I couldn't speak. My eyes told a story that I was unable to write. I wanted Josh to be lying badly but I knew that he wasn't. The way he started to look at me like I belong to him. How he placed his arm around me at the assembly, and how he placed his hand on my lower back and just started to rub it for no reason, gave me goosebumps just mentioning it.

Now, it was Josh's turn to get all smart aleck. "You look like you just saw a ghost." He laughed. "Don't tell me you didn't know?" He said. "Girls know that kind of stuff." He replied. "Okay, I kept my end of the bargain, now it's your turn."

"I saw UCLA in the book cloud that day." I told him.

Josh turned and looked at me real crazy. Now this time, it was him who looked like he had seen a ghost. A month into her heart transplant, Olivia was thriving. I watched her, Mama and Nadine in the kitchen cooking, sipping wine and putting seasoning in the dumplings like nothing.

I watched from a distance listening to whatever pieces of conversation that I could pick up. It was mostly about their kids. What we didn't know, and what we thought we were hiding but they knew anyway. They laughed from experience and cooked like women who had lived and had grown to love the life they had been given.

I had hoped to grow up and to be a combination of them. For my daughter to watch me and the friendships I had forged with the women in my life like they had in theirs. Watching them I could see that they were a recipe that didn't happen often in life. In them, I could see Olivia's recipe for healing. I could see love, hope, and a faith that could move any mountain.

Through the three of them, you couldn't help but hear God's voice and see faith working through all of us to help Olivia. I had struggled with my first story with the new column I had been given. I was beginning to worry about if I would even be able to produce a story at all, now I had one. The trick now would be to convince Olivia "AKA" Moose to take a raincheck on dinner.

CHAPTER SEVEN

PERFECT LOVE

"There is no fear in love; but perfect love cast out fear because fear has torment. But he who fears has not been made perfect in love."

EVERYTHING GOD DOES IS INFLUENCED BY LOVE. CREATION IS A direct result of God's fondness, and his affection to all things that he constructed. Love is so much larger than we are. It has the power to heal any disease, any broken relationship, any financial hardship, **"ANYTHING!"** Love is the secret ingredient that can make enemies become friends.

Love is without judgement. When it chooses to enter into our space, we cannot dictate how, where, or when it will direct its powerful element to restore what has been damaged. In order to receive all of loves benefits, we must be willing to be open. We must be willing to be vulnerable, and we must reserve judgement and allow its force to truly and completely have its way.

When love is able to be free and come into a territory of surrender where the spirt waits on it, the "impossible" becomes "possible," and the influence of the universe shows up and surprising events unfold. See love is not puffed up. Doesn't need fanfare, doesn't need an Oscar, or a

Grammy. All it needs, all it will ever need is willing hearts, open hearts that are willing to trust its power over fear. **"For God has not given us the spirit of fear, but of power, and of love and of a sound mind." 2nd Timothy 1:7**

Fear cannot dwell where love is because it torments. It makes you second guess your power and blinds you from the truth. You cannot trust your direction. You cannot trust your faith. Nor the whispers of God that speak to you every day and provide you with comfort and instruction towards a destiny that only belongs to you.

At 14, I feared lots of things. I also loved many things too. I knew love as family, Mama, Daddy, siblings, Josh, and books. As I think back on it now, the open book in the cloud was teaching me to not just be open to love, but to share it since I was blessed with so much of it.

The path behind the open book offered a way to get to the people that the universe had meant for me to get to. A road to situations, and challenges in which "perfect love" would need to be demonstrated by me at first and the commissioned group of strangers that would in turn recycle it back to me. When I first learned of Olivia's illness, I just wanted to help Moose and his family the way I would want some to help if it were me. Fear did not dare show its ugly face on my radar. If it had, then I would have stomped it so deep into the earth that the universe would have had to vomit it up.

The fear that would later show up was surprising to say the least. The love that had gone into helping Olivia get better had caught blaze like a wildfire on a mission. Sometimes I think I may have shared a little too much love because now Moose was throwing all kinds of love balls my way. To my "fears", it was getting bigger and stronger. Being completely honest, I was becoming exhausted, and I wondered how much more I could take, and how much longer I could run from Moose all because I allowed fear its own space and surrendered to it.

The article was coming along. But to get there, I had to interview Olivia at least a dozen times. I had to become a shadow at Mooses' house and Moose always found away to make his presences felt when I was interviewing his mother. Josh had suggested that I have lunch with him at school just Moose and me. Dumb I thought and I told him so. Kids in high school were just nosey young adults with laundry list of gossip just for the sake of dishing out dirt.

I didn't want to have lunch with Moose at school, at his house, or wherever, I just wanted to write my articles, enjoy what was left of my freshmen year, and not have Moose gaze at me all the time, or make any excuse to get where I was no matter what it took. I had learned by watching that the law of any upper class men, or woman dating beneath their ranks was a bald face lie. Recently it seemed every new couple forming was an upper class man hooked up with a freshman, or a sophomore. Citrus Yard, a girl who I had went to King Junior High with, and a girl who lived in my hood across the street, had gotten the attention of Miles Garrett, a Junior on the Varsity basketball team who was a baller. Within an exhale, she was taking Jazmine's place in popularity and gaining her followers.

Citrus was down. I liked her a lot. She and I clicked instantly. She spoke it to the universe that when she attended Malcolm that she was going to be the girlfriend of a junior or senior with bump. Certain girls at King laughed at her and she went back at them prophesizing about them dating underclass men or having no dating life at all. Like the universe heard her, it came out just like she said and worst. Now, they were all dating pee greeners from King.

We ran into each other at breaks and lunch. She was a hugger, and she was loud, acting like she had never seen Josh or me before. It made me laugh and it pinched Josh's invisible nerves. To escape her, he would stand in line at the snack counter and order us cookies and milk. Plain milk for him and chocolate for me and Snickerdoodles for the both of us.

Like she had some big old secret, she scooted close, smack me on the side of my thigh and lowered her voice so only I could hear it. Then, she gave me an earful. "Girl are you stupid? Moose is fine and I got word, Miles word that he is ape sh…crazy about you."

I didn't half know what to say to "Cit." I had heard a softer version from Josh and in all truthfulness, I had gotten the gaze, rubs, and the touch from Moose himself. I had the articles to write and revise. On top of that I had yearbook, and I was working after school three days a week in the Farmer's Market. What time did I have for a social life? Besides I was scared of falling for him and him dumping me for someone else.

"Cit, I got a lot on my plate right now. I…" said before she cut me off.

"Girl everybody knows that you're this superstar who just happens to have a column at one of the largest newspapers in the country. Okay, I get that. You're on yearbook, and you work after school three days a week. I get that too and I'm too proud of you. But Moose is a damn good catch, and at the end of the day, he ain't caring what you got going on." She said, blowing on her manicured nails. "You helped saved his mama, and whether you like it or not, you're his. It's just a matter of time you know." She grinned.

Before I could further defend myself, Moose, Miles, and Josh were headed over to our table. My heart sunk in my throat, chest, and stomach. Josh hunched his shoulder's as if to say he had no control over Moose following him back to our table. The heck he did. I cut my eyes at Josh and all he did was laugh. It was Moose who handed me my chocolate milk, and cookies, and parked his athletic body right next to me.

He opened my milk, placed my straw in it and handed it to me. I took a few sips and prayed that I wouldn't choke. I could hardly eat my cookies for him staring at me. My nerves were crazy, and I had to say something before they burst.

"So…" I said.

"So, why do you keep avoiding me?" He replied.

"Me, avoiding you," I finished one of my snicker doodles. "Why would I do that?" I said.

"I don't know?" He said. "Why would you?" Scooting even closer to me.

"Maybe that's how it seems, but it's only because I'm kinda busy right now." I said.

"Too busy for me," he said, gazing into my eyes like I was really his already, and like he was scolding me nicely for doing it.

"No," I said. "Moose come on now." I poked him in the side.

"Okay, okay." He smiled and placed his strong, soft hand inside of mines. "So, this means that you'll help me with my essay tonight at my house because you know I suck at writing." He kissed my hand and I just about died.

"Yeah, sure." I said not looking at Josh nor Cit.

"Anything special you want for dinner tonight?" He said, his hand still inside of mines.

"Anything chicken will work." Josh said, finishing his milk.

"Shut up Josh." I said half laughing, half embarrassed.

"It's okay." Moose laughed. "You can have anything you want."

"It's fine." I said. I cut my eyes at Josh again.

The bell rang and I breathed a sigh of relief. Moose tossed my empty milk cartoon and cookie bags in the trash and took back my hand although I was trying to avoid that. He placed his hand in mines again and whispered softly in my ear. "Can I walk you to class?"

"Yeah," I replied. My voice as shaky as colt trying to walk at birth.

The wink of Cit sent my heart racing at a blazing speed I couldn't control. I just wanted to run anywhere and get the hell out of there. But I couldn't. Something greater than my fear refused to allow me to run. I fought it. But it fought back. I fought harder but it came back at a strength that was unmatched to mine. Funny it used who I was afraid of to not just calm my nerves but soothe my rattled spirit.

Moose seemed to know that I was nervous as sin. So, as the on-lookers, gossiper's, beat reporters, pep squad, the entire football team, and everyone else took their turns getting snooping looks in, Moose gently lead me to a hidden corner behind our little theater. He placed his forehead next to mines and placed his strong hands on my waist and begin rubbing my sides like he did at the assembly. Our eyes met, and instantly, I could see what Josh, Cit, and his mother Olivia already knew.

"You, okay?" He asked, never taking his eyes from me.

"Everybody's watching us Moose." The 14 year old spoke.

"Ignore them." He grinned. "People gawk at what they want and will never have." He hugged me, then just held me.

He placed his hand back inside of mines and walked me to class. The crowd had dispersed and the nerves with them. At the door he was a gentleman, He tenderly pulled me into him and hugged me like I had belonged to him since the beginning of time. He kissed my cheek, then my forehead softly, opened the door, then mouthed. "See you tonight."

Later that evening as we sat on my back porch, I laid into Josh. In a girl's world, he had gotten the stupid gene. With Moose, he had suddenly gotten selective Alzheimer's and it wore on my nerves like bad rubber on a tire. You would have thought that Josh would have spoke up for himself in his defense, he didn't. His defense was guilty laughter, and a "you're not letting me explain my side of the story", like he had one.

I hissed, exhaled, and rolled my eyes like a grown woman on a mission. Still Josh was unfazed. Truth be told, I was madder at myself than I could have ever been upset with Josh. Moose had gotten into my sacred space that only I dwelled, and he had no business there. I wasn't ready for the kind of love that Moose was exhibiting. The kind of love that's perfect and did not fear.

It tripped me up how Moose kept coming and with some much confidence. I was scared, and Moose was a young man with an old soul who somewhere along the line had been taught patience. Taught to wait on things, and at the right time love would bloom. I suppose one day I would be perfect in love. That I would be able to feel all that Moose was filling in his heart for me, but at 14, I could not. At least that's what my head was telling me.

I dodged the hammock for my room. The article was my escape from the craziness that had invited itself into my life. I paused briefly and I wondered if the open book that I had seen in the clouds that day had any of this written in it? It had given me so little in the beginning, now so much was happening, things I would have never dreamed. I was beginning to feel that the book in the clouds was my story and that each day of my life I was writing a page.

I started back writing on the article again. The thought of Olivia being alive, well, and completely recovered was nothing less than a miracle. I was proud to share her story, the communities' story and how we all came together in a simple act of love, and how fear was obsolete. I started back working on the article and I lost track of time.

In an instant, I had forgot about helping Moose with his essay. All of a sudden, my eyes landed on the clock on my laptop, and I leaped up like I was putting out a fire. I showered quick and changed my clothes, placed my hair in a messy bun that worked with my cute mini dress and my red jean cover up. I placed my laptop in my bag on my shoulder and exhaled.

In my room was a tall mirror that laid comfortably against the corner of my wall. I passed it, then pivoted back. In looking at myself, I decided that it was too much. It was an essay I was helping Moose with. It wasn't a date. As I was about to change clothes, the front doorbell rang, and from my room I could here Mooses' voice at the door.

"Oh Damn," I said.

"Baby," Mama said. "Moose is here for you. Don't keep this young man waiting."

"Don't have time to change," Sett raised her voice loud enough so Mama and Moose could hear it and laughed.

"Shut up Sett." I said laughing myself.

I quickly put back on my cover-up and nearly bumped into Mama in the hallway. She paused looking at me. Her eyes showed approval at what I was wearing by the sparkle and the smile that came from her lips. She fiddled with my hair and messed with my bang. I never understood why she did that to me at 14. At six it was cool, cute even. But at 14, I thought I was a woman and frowned miserably when she did it.

Sett and Moose were engaged in their own conversation and laughing about upper class stuff. The moment I walked in and Moose saw me, his whole world seemed to stop. It was totally embarrassing how he stared at me. It was like Mama, and Sett weren't even in the room. When he came down from mars, he stood in front of me gazing and said. "Wow! You look beautiful."

"Thanks." I said, nervous again. But I wouldn't dare show it in front of Sett. Mama was different. She was a real woman, and she would understand.

"Mrs. Betts," Moose said, opening the door for us. "What time would you like her home?"

Mama smiled impressed and crossed her arms. "10:30pm will due." She winked at me.

My mouth dropped. I had a 9 o'clock curfew through the week. Eleven on Friday's and Saturday's, and that was only because I was at football games with Josh, Sett, my eldest sister Zuri, and Zuri's best friend Sarabi. If it were just Josh and I, Nadine and Mama agreed that we could be out until 10 o'clock on weekends. The smile on Mooses' face was enormous. I was surprised that he was able to get his head out of the front door.

Olivia greeted me with a hug and a kiss on the cheek. She had prepared a space for us in their indoor room. The table setting was beautiful, purposely set for two. A fresh mixed bouquet of flowers, blended with Sunflowers which made it a perfect garland. The plates were a periwinkle blue. The napkins and silverware matched. Tall blue candles were impeccably lit and as we sat, she happily served us chicken and dumplings, my favorite.

"You didn't have to do this." I said. "I could…"

"You sweet pea will do no such thing." She said. "You will sit here with my son and enjoy this meal." She replied. "By the way," she said. "You look lovely."

"Thank you." I said.

"Holler if you need anything." She said and left.

"You look great you know." He said again, spreading a napkin across his lap.

"Thanks." I blushed.

"So, tell me about this essay." I said and began eating, stunned I could even eat with the way Moose was eyeing me.

Moose swallowed some of his dumplings, wiped his mouth with a napkin, then held up the book David Copperfield, by Charles Dickens. The look on his face said everything, and for some reason it made me laugh.

"What," he said, scooting even closer to me. "I hate this book." He ate more of his food. "I really hate it."

"This is so good." I said, drinking chilled apple cider. "It's a great book Moose." I said, wiping my mouth. "You can't hate David Copperfield. Charles Dickens is a brilliant writer. His books equate to a common theme, poverty." I said as I continued eating.

Briefly Moose lost his gaze, as his eyes show cased shock and awe at my love first and knowledge of an author I admired. His look made me laugh all over again. Olivia, who looked robust and healthy appeared in the indoor room again and asked if we wanted more food, or were we ready for dessert. Moose had another serving. I was saving room for dessert for later.

I complimented Olivia on dinner, and she beamed like a star showing out in the night sky. She looked new, resilient, and so full of life. I prayed that the article that I was writing on her would speak to her journey and offer hope. Moose and I cleared the table. But before we could placed the dishes in the dishwasher, his father Noah shooed us away.

We grabbed a corner next to the cozy fireplace that was lit just right. It wasn't too hot, but just right for a fall evening that had suddenly turned chilly. I reached over Moose and picked up his book David Copperfield and held it like it meant something special and it did. Moose looked at me and shook his head with a smile. He placed his hand to the side of his cheek and just stared at me.

"I think you like that book more than me." He said smiling.

"Moose, it's a great book. I can't believe you don't like it." I looked at him. "Anyway," I said. "Can I see your syllabus?"

He handed it to me and pointed to the points that Mr. O'Malley wanted the class to write on.

"Okay, so what did you get out of the book?" I asked.

"Nothing." He laughed and continued to gaze at me.

"Moose," I laughed. "Come on now. Something had to have gotten your attention?"

"I'm telling you nothing." He raised up. "Nothing, it doesn't even make sense." He scooted even closer to me. So close that I could feel his breath on my cheek and his thigh plastered next to mines.

"Okay," I said, turning my body slightly towards him. "So, tell me what you didn't like, and before you say everything, give me one thing." I replied, trying hard not to look in his eyes.

"If I give you one thing," he said. "Will, you give me a kiss?" His lips touched my ear.

"No." I said. "This is an essay about David Copperfield not about kissing."

"We can make it about kissing if you want?" He said, touching my ear with his lips again.

"Moose," I swallowed hard. "Your essay is due on Monday." I scooted away from him, and he slide his body next to mines.

"We got the weekend." He said, looking deeply into my eyes.

"We have right now." I tried to be firm.

"One kiss." He kissed me on my cheek. "It will stimulate my mind." He said, kissing my cheek softly again.

I took a deep breath and did something that shocked me until this day. I turned towards Moose and looked him straight into the eye and said. "You asked me to help you with your essay so I'm here. You not liking the book is a good thing because then you can explain why, use his points and compare it to something you do like. Okay."

"So, let me get this straight," he said. "If we knock this out then maybe I…"

"Moose, time is ticking." I got bold enough to redirect his thinking.

Olivia delivered lava cakes that put my nostrils then my stomach in a quandary. We ate, talked about the story and suddenly Moose had gotten on a role. We talked in detail about the novel he detested and from his dislike came an outline, and eventually a completion of the five page essay that had a rough start in the beginning. I took a deep breath and he laughed and found a way to place his hand on my back and began rubbing it.

"What?" I said, looking into his eyes.

"You don't get it do you?" He said, rubbing my shoulders now.

"I get we got your essay done." I said, putting my laptop away.

"I'm crazy about you." He turned my face to him. "There's no other way to say it."

"Moose, I've never even kissed a boy before." I said, not knowing that I gave him his lead way.

He kissed my lips so softly and with so much love that it took my breath away. I stared at him for a moment like I couldn't believe what just happened, and I couldn't. Now, I was really nervous.

"Now you have," he smiled and kissed me again and again. This time more like adult's kiss when they're really in love. "I want you to be my girl." He said. "Make me the happiest guy on the planet by saying yes." He kissed me again.

"What about Jazmine?" I said.

"What about her?" He wrapped his arms around my waist. "I don't want her. I want you."

"Daddy said I can't have a boyfriend until I'm sixteen." I replied, looking into his eyes.

"Guess I'm gonna have to talk to your pop then," he kissed me again.

The thing that I feared caught up with me and captured me. The strangest thing about it was that it used Moose to do it. Moose and I had to have that run in. I'm convinced that if we didn't, Olivia would have died and eventually so would have Moose. I had to be open. I had to forgive and step so far out of my comfort zone to surrender to God's will.

I had to follow a path that was unknown, uncharted and I didn't have time to be scared or worry about what I was doing wasn't going to work out. Fear was as foreign to me as soul food is in Ireland. Yet, when it came to Moose and his affection towards me, fear took hold of me because loving someone outside of my circle was way too scary for me.

Nadine had done it with Booker. She was used to Booker being well for a point then not, then taking him to the hospital again, getting him better for a period and starting the same cycle over again. I watched her like I watched life. When Booker was home and better, the parties stopped, her drinking slowed, and her smile was as bright as the morning sun.

There were times when she would take one of Mama's catalogs and order something nice fitting and show her legs for Booker to see. There were times when just the two of them would sit out on the porch on warm summer nights, talk, and watch the stars. Sometimes I wondered if Nadine was watching her own life unfold up there.

Over the past year, I had a lot of time to think. This entire journey thus far had started with a urge to take a different route back to social studies class. That course changed my life forever and in ways I never would have expected. The story that I so badly wanted to read was now becoming clear. The Book I saw in the clouds that day was more than a story. It was a map, a challenge, leading me to a destination that only I could follow. To a family that needed help and comfort, and to a woman who had prayed for healing.

In the beginning, when I witnessed seeing UCLA in the clouds, I thought it was God answering my young prayer when I asked for him to send me to a university to earn my bachelor's degree. It was so much bigger than that. I didn't recognize it then, but the reason I saw UCLA in the book cloud was because the universe had already answered a woman's prayer of healing who at the time I hadn't met yet. And that he was using a surgeon from UCLA to do it.

The letter that I wrote to Dr. Davis was already preordain, strategically planned, and written by a then 14 year old girl who had the heart to help a friend. It was perfectly orchestrated and perfect in love. After the success of Olivia's surgery and word got out that a letter from a 14 year old kid influenced a great surgeon to perform the surgery, my life would change drastically and it scared the heck out of me.

I went from a no named freshman to having an established identity over night. Fate had done that. With the new notoriety came opportunities I didn't see coming, and a love that terrified me more than any column ever could. It was a lot to deal with for a 14 year old to be thrust into love and the limelight all at once. At this point, in my journey I often wondered if the book cloud had purposely hid this part of my story?

I returned to my hammock, my unofficial "burning bush" not for answers, but just to breathe. For a moment, I thought of nothing. Nor, did I allow my mind to roam. I just laid back into my hammock with my eyes closed experiencing quiet.

At first, I felt the nervousness that seemed to travel through my body like it belonged there. The unwelcomed intruder it was had temporarily sat up shop with no plans to move out. It appeared to get stronger with each breath I took. In the beginning of my silence, I yielded to it, untrained to its tricks and deception. But somewhere within my innocent soul, was a mustard seed of faith and a trust planted with strict orders to mature at the very moment I needed it to bloom.

CHAPTER EIGHT

TRUST IN THE LORD

"Trust in the lord with all thine heart and lean not unto thy own understanding. In all thy ways acknowledge him and he shall direct thy paths." Proverbs 3:5-6

LIFE CAN BE TOUGH TO NAVIGATE IN TIMES OF UNCERTAINTY. When we face turbulence in our soul, we experience a disconnect with our faith, and what we believe. Suddenly our confidence becomes shaken and out of fear we develop a false trust in which we dictate our own path. When fear enters trust, it gives off a negative perception. Therefore, we selfishly move God to the back, his plans to the rear, and allow the enemy to convince us that what we are doing will not work out.

When it doesn't work the way we assumed it would, we grab hold to frustration and anger and creep back to God. Trust is a spiritual relationship that people of faith have with God. In this bond, there is no fear, no worry, no second guessing on the promise that has already been confirmed. Trusting in God is to have confidence, faith, and believe that whatever the problem he can solve it. What you need to understand is that God sees the bigger picture and he knows what lies ahead.

In the spring, I turned 15. Two months later summer rolled in. And though my age said I was a teen, my body said otherwise. To my surprise I had gotten taller. I had gotten breast that grew several cup sizes. My hips had gotten wider which had given shape to my buttocks, my thighs had thicken and my entire body transformation gave Moose fits.

I still couldn't understand his interest or affection for me. It was new sometimes scary, and I will admit it kept me up sometimes at night. I thought of Jazmine, Roxanne, Felisha, and others who appeared as though they were born women as far as there physic was concerned. Up until now, I was a girl on an island of women who seemed as if they knew how to bring there "A" game with guys consistently.

I questioned myself constantly why a guy like Moose would be so interested in me, so understanding, so loving, and so genuine. It was at times hard to believe. When I thought, he was going to do anything contrary, he just kept being Moose. When he felt me pulling away. He pulled me right back.

He was the most determined, and stubborn guy I had seen. Josh didn't count. Sometimes I felt that he could read my heart and my thoughts all at the same time, and that's what scared me. What was odd was in all of this was my Mother. She was as staunch about me being 16 years old when I waltzed into the dating world as Daddy. But I don't know what it was about Moose, but she made an exception, and worked on daddy to bend. Obviously, so was Moose, that I didn't see coming.

Moose had turned eighteen and that made Daddy real nervous. I'd hear him and Mama discuss it behind their bedroom door, and any place they felt I wasn't. I'd hear my older sister Sett laugh at their discussions, and my eldest sister Zuri side with Mama and Daddy firing back on her and reminding her that she was sixteen before she started dating. Zuri would laugh, turn, and face him and say. "Yeah, daddy, but she's not me. Me is very mature for her age. What's a year?"

"What I've been trying to tell him." Mama joined in, in agreement. "Moose is a good young man. He's got a good head on his shoulder, works hard with Noah in the family business, which is gonna be his someday, I'm sure." She said, seasoning the roast. "He's a good soul, and you know he reminds me of you."

Daddy was daddy. "The boy's eighteen." He peeled potatoes. "A boy that age has his hormones going all over the place. I've been there I know, and I don't trust it. Have either of you looked at our daughter and your baby sister lately?"

"It's called maturity baby." Mama said to Daddy and laughed. "Mama used to call it filling out. Your baby is growing up, and you are going to have start trusting her." Mama kissed Daddy and he blushed and lit up like a million lights on a Christmas tree.

Josh had filled out as well. I noticed his man coming on when we went from carrot tops to freshmen. But now it was full blown. He was much taller so much taller, that I had to look up at him and get up on my tippy toes to smack his face when we were messing around with each other. He was always cute, but now he was handsome. A manly handsome that drove girls wild, and they had begun lining up for him like he was some rockstar.

He bit like a fish to water, and his phone blew up like popcorn in a skillet. I watched them sit in the bleachers and watch him take down opponents like an eagle swallowed his prey. They didn't follow tennis. They followed him.

They bought him lunch. Madison Palmer, a varsity cheerleader slid a fifty dollar Pietro's gift card in his locker. She had discovered Josh's love for pizza and lasagna and had hoped to tempt him with a date. Madison was one of the nicer cheerleaders. She wasn't stuck up like Jazmine and she didn't treat freshman like they were dirt and bird crap. Her smile was genuine and when she spoke to you it wasn't fake, or like you owed her something. But she wasn't Josh's type.

Felisha Gibson was a mess. She was the captain on pom squad, and she thought she was it. She had a new boyfriend every week always another sucker waiting in line just to say that he had a twirl with her.

She was pretty with a nice body, and popular with the guys for the wrong reason. She'd brag in the quad how she couldn't keep a guy more than a week because they became clingy and needy, and she needed her independence.

She made me laugh. But most girls hated her. Her parents were wealthy. She drove her brand new Porsche to school every day, and she inherited a group of groupies without any effort. She had decided to put her claws into Josh. She had rumors going around school that he wouldn't last a week with her and that after three days, he'd beg her to take him back. I laughed at that to because I knew that she didn't know Josh.

To my surprise, she invited Josh and me to her house for a party over the weekend. Daddy surprised me by saying I could go if Josh was going, and that I had to be home at 11 o'clock. Mama persuaded him to midnight. He agreed and then objected to every outfit I tried on. Mama had to intervene again. Josh showed up with a girl from our hood whose name was Kia. Kia was tall, not boney, but shapely and was confident in who she was. She wore her hair in Jumbo braids and tossed it in an updo, and she looked illustrious.

Zuri had picked my outfit and since it was summer, she bought me a befitting mini dress that was a bold red Kenta print with spaghetti straps that showed all of my new maturity, and Moose couldn't see straight. He held onto me like I was rare gold, and he let every guy there know except for Josh that I was his by the way he held me. The way he stole kisses from me in hidden corners would have made Daddy freak.

I noticed Felisha's reaction of Josh and Kia firsthand. It was like she was hit in the face with a crowbar. Her light skin turned a pale red. Her eyes bulged out like something, or someone had scared the mess out of her, and her mouth trembled like she was about to break out with the ugly cry. Josh was a great dancer and so was Kia. The way they danced looked like they were in love and that they were the only two in the world.

Moose nearly passed out. So did his squad of ballers who had come to adore Josh. It was at that point that I caught Jazmine's eye. Her look was hateful a look in waiting to destroy me because I had taken something that she wanted badly, and amongst her peers I made her look like a fool. Sadly, that was her vision, and her story.

Her venom swept through my body like a frost on a wintry day and her eyes told me that she had plans. After the party, Jazmine was out for blood. She focused on me like a camera on a subject. The way I dressed, wore my hair, my extra curricula activities, my classes, my column, my family, my everything, you name it. She was out to destroy me because in her small mind, I had taken something that never belong to her in the first place.

Moose was her goat and my king. But she refused to see it or acknowledge it. Beyond being stuck on stupid, she was blinded by a lie that presented itself as truth, and she was hell bent on revenge.

Moose on the other hand was hell bent on wearing Daddy down and was beginning to get on his invisible nerves. He helped Daddy reseed our lawn, plant his vegetable garden, strip the old fence, and put up a brand new one. And he insisted on helping Daddy design and build a long awaited promise that Daddy had made to me at the age of nine; a grown up tree house. It made Mama laugh and Daddy shake his head at her and Moose. In the cool of the evening, he served her coffee and teacakes on the front porch as they watched the sun go down.

Zuri said that they had been doing that since forever. It was their time away from the craziness. Time to talk about married people stuff, laugh, love, and of course for Daddy, to vent about Moose.

"You know that boy that calls himself liking our daughter, think I don't know what he's doing." He sipped coffee and looked at Mama.

"Well, I think it's cute." Mama said, sipping her coffee. "He's trying to show you who he is. How much he loves our daughter, and how far he's willing to go for her." Mama laughed as if she remembered some of the stunts that Daddy pulled. "Um," Mama said, biting into one of Daddy's irresistible teacakes. "Baby, you need to market these."

"You think?" He looked at Mama. "I've been thinking about building us a bakery, a diner of some sort on the back end of our property when I retire and sell them and some of Grandmama's other dishes and desserts." He looked into the stars as if it were a part of God's plan.

"I think that's wonderful baby." Mama said.

"Been thinking about it a lot, almost as much as this damned Moose." He said. "Boy is working on my nerves. I have never seen a young man so determined to be with a girl in my life." He sighed, then bit into a teacake. "You think she ready. You think she can really handle having a guy in her life right now?"

"Yes," Mama said. "Yes, I do." She took another sip of her coffee. "Do you trust her?"

"Who, my baby girl?" He replied. "I do." He said. "But he's 18, and my little girl is only 15. I'm not gonna lie to you, as a man and as her father, I worry." He said. "I know she's smart. I know she's got a good head on her shoulders, but she likes that boy." He paused and looked at Mama. "I just want her to grow up, have a great life and live the life that God intended for her to have."

"She's already living it baby." Mama rubbed Daddy's head. "Just trust her and be there when she needs her dad."

That seemed to have soothed Daddy's spirit. He took Mama's hand in his and held it like he was holding time. They sat silent, watching the stars and in that moment, time had escaped them. I could only hope that Daddy would cut Moose and I a solid and allow us to have a normal relationship without sneaking.

During my sophomore summer I was being tested in ways that made me learn, and trust God's timing, direction, and not lean on my small, minded understanding. My test came through an enemy whose sole purpose was to destroy not just me, but who God was creating me to become. Jazmine Brothers had a crazy kind of love for Moose. A craziness I hadn't seen.

In the beginning, it looked like they were perfectly paired for each other. She was always around in the quad with Moose and his entourage, laughing at his jokes, gawking at him like a lovesick puppy. I assumed that they were a couple and nobody at Malcolm was saying anything different. I was new, unknown, and a freshman, and I didn't know much about the kids who went to Malcolm except for my sister Sett, Josh's sister Ruth, and some of the homies from the neighborhood.

It's hard for me to remember if she paid any attention to me or not. More than likely, not. Freshmen were at the bottom of the food chain which meant we got no respect unless we were bold enough to demand it. I was one of the bolder ones, which is how I got acquainted with Moose.

To my recollection, Jazmine was eye candy to all the guys, and envied like hell by the girls with a few exceptions, me, Cit, and my sister Sett being a small handful of them. Figure wise, she was a woman through and through, and it drove the guys wild. She was arrogant, cocky, and way too sure of herself. Being at the bottom of the food chain, I knew that I was not on her radar. I doubt seriously that she even knew I was a student at Malcolm.

She never said hello or greeted me with a smile. I was invisible to her until Moose had a sudden interest. All of a sudden, she began paying me attention, speaking to me, trying to recruit me to try out for pep squad, and to my dismay, she started studying me in a way that made the tiny hairs on my flesh stand at attention. When she couldn't sway Moose away from me, she became venomous.

Something in my gut told me that she was out for blood. Moose had risen to be the top linebacker in the state. Our Friday night football games were no longer played at our field, Moose drew crowds from everywhere, and suddenly Malcolm was playing football games at the Pavilion Stadium, our local University. Scouts came from everywhere.

Every University wanted him, even some NFL scouts came out to watch this linebacker with the Midas touch.

All it took was for the University of Michigan to be the fly on the wall at Mooses' house continuously. The head coach having Sunday dinners, and his coaching staff working out with Moose at the Pavilion and Jazmine went to work. I didn't think much of it at first. After Olivia's story, my column caught fire. The stories I was writing were touching hearts and penetrating souls. I was getting letters from everywhere.

Daddy had bent his strict dating law and allowed me and Moose to be declared official and Moose nearly lost his mind. We celebrated on top of his barn roof, kissing like crazy, getting a little naughty and watching shooting stars fly across the night sky. Life was good, until Jazmine got in the way. Jazmine was a regular at the farmer's market in the beginning. She would come to the "Farmer's Market" in the morning purchasing fruits and veggies and making small talk with Mr. Ward. In the afternoons, she parked herself a seat right on the "50 yard line" and watched Moose train like he was already a part of the University of Michigan squad. A malicious grin cruised across her face, and like a black widow, she moved in for the kill.

Our last month of summer she struck. She spun her lie in the beauty shop at first acting like Moose had given her first dibs and that she was his girl. Like a snowball gaining speed, the lies blossomed. Soon everybody was talking about Moose and his commitment to the University of Michigan. My column was blazing. My readers were thrilled with my stories and my editor was electrified by the results.

I was burning the midnight oil and focused on making each article better than the next. Josh called me a zombie living off words. I laughed and kicked his but in a bicycle race on our way to work at the Farmer's Market. We raced in, put on our aprons, and went to work unpacking produce. We weren't there fifteen minutes before Mr. Ward made it a point to spread the news about Moose.

"Looks like Moose is headed to the University of Michigan." He said proud. "He's going pro now." He grinned.

My mouth dropped and my eyes nearly leaped out of my sockets. This couldn't be right. Moose hadn't even started his senior year at Malcolm. If it were true, he certainly would have made sure that he told me about it. I was numb and instead of asking Moose about it. I assumed by my own understanding that the lie that Jazmine had woven was true.

"Who told you that?" Mr. Ward, I said, trying to act all calm.

"His little girlfriend." He smiled. "Cute little thang, Felisha, Karen, I don't know what the child's name was, but she told me." He said. "She better put her claws in that boy before some other young Philly does."

If Josh hadn't caught me, I swear I would have fell. Moose not only lied to me, but he was playing on me, and acting like he was so in love with me. At 15, I had suffered my first interruption in a relationship that scared me from the onset. What I had feared came upon me and disguised itself as truth.

I rushed out back behind the warehouse and gasp to catch my breath. I cried so hard until my chest began to hurt. In the present, I hated Moose, and I wanted nothing else to do with him. Mr. Ward seemed surprised at my reaction to his news.

He looked at Josh strange. "Did I say something Son?

"Nah, Mr. Ward," he lied. "She's got a lot on her shoulders right now. Let me go talk to her." He said.

Josh placed an arm around my shoulders and just let me cry. I felt comfort just laying on his shoulder sobbing. Whether he disagreed with me or not, he understood and he knew in the moment I was hurt.

"Hey," he said. "You know Moose would never lie to you, and damn straight he would never cheat on you." He replied. "I've gotten to know him and he's a righteous dude, and from a man's perspective, he can't even see straight when it comes to you."

"Why would Mr. Ward say it then?" I said, lifting my head from off his shoulder.

"Adults say things Me; you know that. It's just gossip. People read into things. They see Moose working out with UM, and the chatter starts. I don't believe a word of it, and you shouldn't either." He said.

"What about the girls?" She said. "You believe that's a lie?"

"Bonafide." He said. "You're a writer and you write for one of the most prestigious papers in the country. Even, though you write about inspiration, don't you have to get the facts first?" He replied.

"That's a paper." I said defeated, not letting him know.

"What's the difference?" He snickered, pissing me off. "Go talk to Moose and stop assuming."

CHAPTER NINE

LET'S US NOT BE WEARY

*"And let us not be weary in well doing: for in due season,
we shall reap if we faint not. Galatians 6:9*

ALL PEOPLE OF FAITH HAVE EXPERIENCED A SPIRITUAL DEPRES-sion. The enemy prides itself on discouraging those of faith when we are doing good and being of service. This attack seems to occur when we are on the right path and when we are growing, at the top of our game and doing the will of God. Without warning, comes the nails, the thorns, then the boulder that shakes our foundation and causes our temporary struggle to appear hopeless.

Here is where you sink or swim. Here is where you are on the verge of collapse, but the spirit of God inside of you will not allow you to faint. This force in your soul is like a place of the strength inside of your heart that awaits the timing of your due season. Every nail will be reverted into hanging up troubles that got in your way. Each thorn used to remove each unwanted guess, and every boulder to retain a wall of protection.

You see, what seemed like your path of instability, uncertainty, and hostility, was strategically orchestrated by God, using what appeared to work against you as for you. ***Ecclesiastes 3:1*** says, *"There is a time for everything, and a season for every activity under the heavens."* This means that every circumstance that we go through in this life is not by accident. These incidents are uniquely designed by God deliberately for a greater goal.

At 15, you don't know this. Every emotion that scratches the surface of your heart gets taken to the next level. Teens are sponges of energy that are untrained at how to deal with matters of the heart especially when it falls to the low scale of rumors that hide behind the truth. That being said, I lit into Moose without any substance of fact behind what I had heard and what I had talked myself into believing. Temporarily Jazmine was on top of the world.

My young emotions had gotten the best of me. When Moose came over, I refused to see him. When he called, I wouldn't talk to him, and when he text, I would not answer. Poor Moose was thrown into a storm where he didn't belong, and it affected him miserably. He worked long hours in his father's shop. He worked out hard, stop hanging out with his boys, and when he did eat dinner, he ate alone in his room.

Olivia had noticed his change and couldn't stand it any longer. She ignored her husband Noah's advice about giving him his space. Something was wrong and she had grown impatient waiting for her son to spill his guts. He looked up from sanding a table and there she was with her hand on her hip.

"Mom," he said. "What are you doing here?"

"Funny," she pulled down a chair and sat. "I was about to ask you the same thing."

"I work here, and these table setts are not going to build themselves." He said, barely looking up at her.

"You listen to me." She said and pulled the plug from his sander. "Sit your butt down." She said. "I know my son. There is something very wrong with you and whether you like it or not. You are going to tell me what it is, and whatever it is we are going to figure it out and deal with it together."

He exhaled and ran his fingers through his wet, curly hair. "I don't even know where to start." His eyes were sad and teary.

"The beginning is a start." She said, sitting closer to him.

"It's Me," he said. "She's not speaking to me, and she accused me of going behind her back dating other girls and making a commitment to UM when that's the furthest thing from my mind." He fought back the tears. "I don't even know where she's getting this from."

"Oh, sweet boy." She took him in her arms and held him. "Hey." She said, still holding him as if he wore the eight year old needing a hug from his Mommy. "It will be okay. You know how much she loves you." She looked at him. "Talk to her."

"Mom, I've tried." He blinked away the tears. "And she just won't talk to me. I don't know what to do." He said, shaking his head.

Meka's mother Imani had noticed the same thing when it came to her daughter's behavior. She was on the same frequency as Olivia, except, Josh beat her to point. Josh ran across the grass, open the Betts front door, tossed a hand at Imani and went directly to Meka's room. He didn't even knock as he usually did. He just barged right in.

"Josh," I turned to face him. "What is wrong with you? Can't you see I'm working. And don't you ever knock." I said smart mouthed.

"No Me," he said. "What the hell is wrong with you? Moose is a good guy and he doesn't deserve this." He fumed. "Don't you get it. Somebody is out to sabotage you and Moose, and you're so damn caught up into being mad at him that you haven't thought to use your reporting skills and find out the facts."

"What, so you're Mooses' spokesperson?" I said.

"Somebody needs to be because you're certainly not." He said. "I love you Me. I do. Do you honestly think that I would just let any guy come into your space and your heart like that if I didn't trust that he was good for you?" He sighed. "I've had it with you. Either you talk to Moose and hear his side or…"

"Or what," I turned and stood.

"Or don't even bother coming over anymore," he said and slammed the door.

I was flabbergasted and my mouth dropped to the floor. Josh and I had never once had a fight and he never went against me for anybody. My body shook like a frigid chill in the winter. My eyes flooded with tears and the article I was writing for my column was put on hold. I opened my side door and ran to my hammock and burst out crying.

Mama had witnessed Josh slamming my bedroom door and charging out of the house like a frustrated man on a mission. She slipped on her shoes and was headed out back where I was. But Daddy stopped her and came out to the hammock and laid in it with me. He gathered me in his arms like he did when I was a little girl and held me. He kissed me on the forehead and said. "What's the matter with Daddy's baby?" He placed his cheek to my forehead.

"Josh is upset with me because I'm mad at Moose and I won't talk to him." I cried. "And he doesn't want me to come around anymore." I wept.

"Josh is upset with you over Moose." Daddy sounded confused at first. "Well, this is a first. Josh has been lying for you and getting in trouble for you since he was born." He snickered.

"Not true," I said, still laying on Daddy's shoulder.

"Your version not mines," he chuckled. "So, tell me why you are mad at Moose."

"Because he lied to me about going to University of Michigan, and he's cheating." I said. "Everybody's talking about it." I said.

"Well, I'm not talking about it. Your mother's not talking about it. He said. "Did you ask him about all of this?"

"I don't have to." I said, a teenage dumb.

"So, you gonna make your own assumptions according to what?" He said.

"Daddy, you're not being fair." I said looking up at him.

"Okay," he said. "Now, I'm not being fair." He laughed at my teenage knowledge. "With all due respect, that Moose boy made too many trips over here if you ask me to try and talk to you. Too many phone calls, too many text, and you didn't want to talk him. Even I felt sorry for the boy." He laughed. "That's your Mama in you."

"Is not." I said.

"Is so," He replied. "How much did you bug me about breaking my dating rules to be with this boy, and now you don't want anything to do with him." He laughed. "Talk to the boy please so he can stop bothering me." He laughed again. "Baby," he said, "look at me. All kidding aside, never assume anything until you get the facts okay." He kissed my forehead again. "I had my doubts about that boy, but turns out he's a good kid, and he really loves my daughter." He held me longer. "But don't get no funny ideas," he said. "You ain't marrying him and nobody else until you're 30."

"Daddy." I said, looking at him. "You think Josh will stay mad at me?" I asked.

"Josh," he exhaled. "Josh is just blowing off steam. "He has to be holding Moose in high esteem to cross you." He raised an eyebrow. "Josh loves you. He'll be alright." He hugged me.

A hug from Daddy was like a hug from God. He had strengthen me and gave his wisdom and I took it. Mama watched from the back kitchen door and blew a kiss at me. She could tell by my eyes and my smile that sadness had left and Joy had returned. I blew a kiss back. Slipped on my sandals and walked across the yard to Josh's house where Booker was sitting outside reading his evening news paper. Booker looked at me and smiled, and called out for Josh. When Josh didn't answer he told me to go on back with the brightest smile. I kissed his cheek and followed his lead.

Josh was in his room watching music videos. He was a Michael Jackson fanatic and was watching "Thriller," his favorite. I sat on his bed, and he looked up at me and swirled around and offered me some popcorn he had popped.

"Are you still made at me?" I asked taking some popcorn.

"No." He said. "Look," he turned and faced me. "I'm sorry for acting like that and making you cry. I…"

"I'm going to talk to Moose." I said. "How'd you know I was crying?"

"I hid behind our apricot tree, and I saw you talking to Pop. I was going to hop the fence and come over, but he beat me to it." His look was sad.

I kissed his cheek. "Best buds until the end."

"Best buds until the end. And I will never make you cry again, I promise."

"I know." I said. "Can we promise never to fight again.

"Promise." He kissed me on the cheek.

"I gotta go talk to Moose." I said, getting up.

"You okay. Want me to come?" He asked.

"Nah, I got this. Wanna go for chicken and pizza later?"

"Yep," he said. "Let's do it."

"Oh, by the way, I think Kia is a good catch." I winked.

"We're just hitting rounds, nothing serious." He grinned.

"Yeah, but it's about to be." I said and left.

I rode my bike over to Mooses' place. From the front, I could hear the building and making of furniture from the warehouse all the way in the back. Olivia greeted me with a hug. She wrapped her arm around me and took me to the warehouse where the twins, Mr. Gentry and Moose were working.

"Look who I found." She smiled.

The twins waved and smiled goofy grins on their faces and said, "what's up Me."

Moose looked up at me, a sadness in his eyes. "Hey Me." He said and continued to work. Mr. Gentry smiled wide, stopped hammering on a chair he was building and came over to me and gave me the sweetest hug and kiss on the cheek. I walked over towards Moose and said Hi. He returned the hi but little else.

He had never been this cold to me, and it scared me. I cleared my throat and surprised myself when I asked him to teach me how to cut the pattern to the back of the chair he was making. He paused and just looked a me and shook his head. I elbowed him in the side and said, "come on, I'm serious."

"Me," he looked at me. "I'm busy right now."

"Too busy for me." I said, tying on an apron.

He suddenly stopped, laid down his tool and looked at me like I was crazy. "I came by. I called a gazillion times, I texted even more, and you didn't even think enough of me to answer." He said. "I don't even know why you're so mad at me?" He shook his head.

"I'm sorry." I said, scooting ever so close to him. "It was rumored that you were going to UM, and that you were seeing other girls, and…"

He laid his tool again and cut the power off, looked at me and exhaled. "Pop, I need to talk to Me for a minute, I'll be right back." He took me by the hand and nearly pulled me out of the warehouse.

"Let's get one thing straight." He said. "I don't know whose promoting these lies about me, but I'm not going to UM, and I would never cheat on you."

He said. "What's the matter with you? I love you. But you don't seem to get that." He replied. "Why didn't you just come to me?"

I wrapped my arms around his waste and tippy toed to look up at him. "I don't know. Stupid, I guess. I was scared that I might lose you and that…"

"That what," he looked at me. "That I would just up and leave. I would never do that. Me, you have trust me, and you have to talk to me first." He said. "I thought I had lost you. I thought you didn't want to be with me anymore." His eyes grew sad.

I shook my head as I looked into his eyes. "I love you. I…"

Moose stopped my speech dead center with a kiss that nearly knocked me off my feet. When he kissed me, he gave me goosebumps, and made me want to do naughty things with him that Daddy would lose his mind over. Zuri and Mama had talks with me about my body changing and going from a girl to a woman. After that kiss, I knew why.

My fear came to fruition when Mama asked me flat out if I had or thought about doing it with Moose. My mouth opened but no words came out. At least not right away, when they did, I said no and that I hadn't done it with him, nor had I thought about it, which was a ball face lie. I was young and dumb and didn't think it out clearly. The next day we were at the clinic at a BC orientation for young adults.

The lie had cooled and was shelved to collect dust and return to the invisible rumor that it was. Mr. Ward never spoke of it again. Nor did any of the barber shops, beauty salons, and God knows who else had spoke on it, or added to it. I had always wondered who started such a vicious lie and in the back of my mine was a secret prayer wanting the culprit to reveal themselves.

On a Friday, and on a sweltering day in August, Jazmine had returned to the Farmer's Market. Josh and I laughed and joked around in the warehouse, and she and Mr. Ward made small talk in the front. As if time had rolled out the reaping what you sow carpet, the angel of vengeance showed up to answer my secret prayer, out of the blue Mr. Ward paused from bagging her items.

"I knew it." He wiggled his finger. "I knew, I knew you from somewhere." He began bagging again. Jazmine looked at Mr. Ward strange. "Hey Meka, Josh come out here for a minute."

We stopped our horseplay thinking that Mr. Ward was calling on the both of us to assist him in the front. However, to my surprise, it was much bigger than that. we made our way up front and to our surprise there was Jazmine, putting her change and her wallet back in her purse.

"Hi Jazmine." I said, forcing myself to speak. Josh, however, offered up a wave.

"Hi," she looked at me with so much spite in her eyes.

"This is the one I was trying to tell you about, and for the life of me I couldn't think of this child's name for a gold nugget in a bush. This is Moose's girl." He said. "Though I heard he turned down Michigan and others, hang on to that young man. He's going to one of these top schools, and he's going to pro." He handed her, her receipt.

The look in my eyes was dangerous. The look in hers was sheepish, and her body language spelled guilty. Suddenly, she was in a hurry, in rushing out of the market, she ran right into Moose and her items fell and went all over the place. My moment had arrived, and I took it.

"Hey Moose," I said. "Aren't you gonna help your girlfriend pick up her stuff?"

Their eyes met, and like Moose was given the gift of discernment, he immediately knew that she was the perpetrator behind the spiteful gossip that nearly cost him his girl. Before, he could tear into her, she blew out of the market leaving her goods on the floor. The truth is like a map with a soul. connected to a force that is greater than any falsehood slithering like a snake on a mission to inflict poison in innocent veins.

Jazmine's act of maliciousness was not some rare, premeditated act of vengeance to weave her lie into getting the man she so badly wanted. It was intentionally designed and allowed to teach all of us involved a valuable and important lesson. On our paths there will be enemies great as well as small. The greater the blessing, the bigger the enemy. ***If God allows you to be bitten, then he has prepared a serum to heal you. If he allows darkness to overshadow you, then he will bring in a light to free you.***

My due season came through a routine grocery run by a girl that hated my guts all because Moose chose me. The lie that had started there ended there. The truth that was bombarded by darkness, burst through with the brightest of light and revealed the enemy in plain sight. What had bitten me had cured me, and the venom she had spew revealed who she was and branded her character forever.

C H A P T E R   T E N

DETOUR

And it came to pass, when Pharaoh had let the
people go, that God led them not [through] the way of
the land of the Philistines, although that [was] near; for
God said, Lest peradventure the people repent when
they see war, and they return to Egypt: But God led
the people about, [through] the way of the wilderness
of the Red sea: and the children of Israel went up
harnessed out of the land of Egypt. Exodus 13:17-18

DETOURS ARE UNEXPECTED EVENTS THAT ALTER THE COURSE OF our lives. Without warning, the future can come from a totally different direction. However, surprises remind us that we are not in control. God is never thrown off course, rattled, or dumbfounded by trials that make there way in our lives. Despite obstacles, God knows how to maneuver and power his way through.

Take the children of Israel, by all accounts, it made perfect sense for them to move forward by land. For God, it didn't. Going by land presented an unforeseen problem for a wounded nation to try and fight a battle God knew physically or spiritually they could not win. A detour was purposely executed by God for the Jews to go through the wilderness by sea and avoid a dilemma that would not work in their favor.

Sometimes, God will create a diversion on our path and throw us completely off guard. At present, such a digression will no doubt cause alarm and disappointment because the normal route was disrupted. For the life of it we cannot understand why. When it comes to your purpose, and when God has a plan for your life, he will design an alternative route to get you to your rightful place safely and on schedule.

Detours are not all bad. At times, God uses them as a mechanism of protection like he did with the Jews. Diversions may cause you to get flustered and become distraught, but with God in control there is always a method to the madness. Think about it. When driving on a crowded highway, and your GPS redirects you to another route though unexpected, do you not continue to follow. When you arrived safely to your destination, and you discovered that re-routing your original course saved you from something tragic, did it really matter how you got there as long as you got there unscathed?

Time seemed to be in the mood for a speedy marathon. The day as a thousand years was in play. I was a teenager a minute. I blinked and I was 18. The woman that had hid inside my teenage body burst through and took center stage. My thighs had gotten shapelier and flowed perfectly down to my beautiful legs. My behind finally filled out my shorts and jeans, and my Charlies along with the rest of my body drove Moose nuts.

I was a runt when he had developed a fetish for me. I swore he would leave once another mature girl came along that was more advanced in certain areas than I was and was either a junior or senior. It never happened. Moose had witnessed my development at each stage, and his hormones were off the charts. Moose was all over me like chocolate chips to cookie dough. He made it a point to let me know that I was his forever and the way he treated me, I knew he wasn't lying. I found out from Josh that Moose had asked Daddy for my hand in marriage the moment I turned 16.

Of course, Daddy said "no," but Daddy's no had driven Moose, and according to Josh every year after that he continued to ask Daddy for my hand. However, it was always no. Daddy made it quite clear that he would just have to wait until I graduated from college as if he wouldn't try and have another excuse.

Somehow my ears were mute to this, and for some reason Josh conveniently forgot to tell me. Later I would learn that Moose forbade him to tell me until he had gotten a "yes" answer from Daddy. My ears burned for another reason during this time. Mr. Palmer, my high school counselor, and our Principal Mrs. Shoemaker, were pushing for my parents to let me graduate early from high school so I could do the early application process to apply for the University.

Mama was having none of it. In her motherly opinion, she felt that I wasn't ready and needed to stay the course and graduate with my class on time. To my surprise, Daddy disagreed, and this is where it got interesting.

My two older sister's Zuri and Sett agreed with Daddy. Sett was on her way out from UC Berkley, and she was jazzed by the mere fact that her baby sister could graduate a year early and began her official quest into adulthood.

Honestly, both Josh and I had grown tired of the simple drama of high school and had craved something much more adult. Yeah, there were parties, drama, and craziness in college to. But amongst the noise was a door that lead to opportunity. This did not exist in high school. High school was all about discovery and we wanted something more. We spent many star filled nights in our hammock talking about leaving high school, planning it almost, knowing that our new chapter awaited us.

I didn't know it then, but the universe was about to create a detour from what the book cloud had shown me when I was just 13. I had no idea that the diversion I was about to encounter would toss me on my butt and challenge me in ways that I had never been confronted. One day I saw Mama and Daddy's door closed and I knew what that meant. We all knew what it meant. They were talking some serious stuff that their kids weren't privy to, including the older set.

Curiosity had gotten a hold on my rambunctious spirit, and I crept to the forbidden entry, placed my ear softly to the door and listened. The first thing I heard were mumblings between the two of them at first. Then, I heard Daddy.

"Listen suga." Daddy said. "The girl is done with all her school credits and all her requirements. Looks like to me, she would be better suited to having a year of college under her belt then be here with too much time and Moose on her hands." He replied, drinking more of his coffee.

Mama managed to giggle. "Moose is wearing you down, isn't he?" She laughed again.

"He's wearing on my nerves is what he's doing." He replied, then sipped more coffee.

"I thought you liked him, and I thought you were okay with their relationship. Give him credit baby he's courageous, brave, and persistent to keep coming back to you again and again asking like that." She drank more coffee.

"I do like the boy. But my daughter's got a career and a future." He said. "She didn't ask for it to come so soon and like it or not it did." He said. "At 16 years old, she had a syndicated column. College will only help her nurture that."

"Ah," Mama sighed. "She's my baby and I want her to enjoy these years because she can't get them back." She said. "She's so young to have so much on her shoulders already. I don't even think she knows her column is syndicated. Yet, she keeps pushing along. I just don't think she's ready."

"Or is it, your not ready?" Daddy said, finishing his coffee. "She can do it baby. Look what she's done so far. Believe me, she's ready." He kissed Mama.

Mama took a deep breath, looked at Daddy and laid her head on Daddy's shoulder. In that very moment, before she even opened her mouth, I knew in her soul she had said yes. Like a dummy, I sprinted away from my parent's bedroom door as if some real emergency was taking place. For me, it was. I darted across the lawn at lightening speed and hopped up to Josh's top step on the porch and raced into the front door.

Mama, God bless her soul had yelled something out of their bedroom window at me. Whatever it was, I didn't hear it. Knowing her, she was probably scolding me for listening at their door. I ran into Josh's house half winded trying to tell him the good news. He looked at me like I was crazy and signaled with his hands, time out.

"Me." He said. "Slow down. You're going to kill yourself before you spill. Deep breaths." He said, as if he were some kind of therapist.

I took two quick breaths. "Mama said yes. I'm graduating early and now I can apply to college."

Josh grabbed me and wouldn't let me go. Truth was, I actually didn't know if Mama had actually said yes. But it was a feeling that spoke from the depths of my soul, and I believed it. Moose was already on his second year at UCLA, and like the coaches and scouts predicted, he was already making a national name for himself.

I wanted so badly to go to UCLA. Not because of Moose, yes, he was part of it. But I remembered what the book cloud had promised. The first four letters I had seen from the book cloud were UCLA. The catalog in our career center at King was UCLA. Dr. Davis, who operated on Olivia, UCLA, and my boss, Chief Editor of the Gazette was an alum at UCLA.

It already seemed destined, and Mama agreeing for me to graduate early only confirmed it. I was too excited to stroll across the campus that had claimed me long before I thought about any college. The whole notion of me seeing the book cloud in the sky with its cryptic message was starting to make sense and all come together. I felt like the universe was about to unveil the whole story and make it clear as to why it chose me to see it in the first place. Boy was I wrong.

Mama had broken the news to me about her decision to let me graduate early and apply to college in a way that I didn't expect. She came into my room sat next to me on my bed and just looked at me like I was all grown up.

"I want you to know that this decision to let you graduate early and go to the University a year earlier than what I would have wanted was not an easy decision to come to. You are my baby, and no matter how old you get. You will always be my baby girl." She brought me into her arms. "Even though your dad decided long before I did, that you were ready to take that leap into adulthood. It took a bit more praying and listening to God to get where he was." She said. "Something bigger than he and I had decided that the moment you took on the challenge to see to it that Olivia had gotten her transplant, you were ready." She said holding me in her arms. "I know you have lived your entire young life wanting to go to UCLA, but please promise your Mama that you will apply to USC. It's the best journalism school in the country, and I just know in my heart that you will do well there." She replied as she kissed my forehead.

"I promise." I said. How could I say no. Like I was six, I climbed into Mama's lap and held onto her, and I cried hard like the rain I had watch cascade from the clouds days ago.

I met with Mr. Palmer immediately. We sat up a time at the test center to take the SAT. He sat up a couple of workshops prior to the SAT so that I would not only know what to expect on the exam, but that I could learn techniques in taking it so that I could get the highest possible score. I was so excited that I could barely contain myself. Then, the bombshell hit.

"First and foremost, let me just say that I'm extremely proud of you. The Gazette for Pete's sake, a syndicated column, and add USC to the mix and it is one heck of a future." He said. "So, without a doubt, we are applying to USC?" He asked, almost knowing in his mind that I was.

"Actually Mr. Palmer, I was planning on applying to UCLA. I sort of planned for it my whole life." I said.

"Meka." He scooted his chair into the table and looked at me like I said something terribly wrong. "Though I am an alum from USC, and yes I will admit that I've got my biases." He said. "And don't get me wrong, UCLA is a great school, but, well it doesn't have a journalism program."

"But it does have a communications program, and she could just as well major in communications and have a minor in say broadcasting." Mrs. Shoemaker, our principal said, a UCLA alum who yelled from her office.

"Debbie," Mr. Palmer said. "We both want what's best for the child. Meka is well on her way, writing her own ticket, and we both know that USC can only enhance that." He fired back respectfully.

"Are you sure?" I said. "How can they not have a major in journalism? That doesn't make sense. But the book cloud was clear." I said.

"What?" Mr. Palmer looked at me strange. "Book who?"

I realized I was thinking out loud and had never told anyone about the book cloud not even Josh. Anger struck me like a brutal bolt of lightning and overwhelmed me like a fierce enemy on a mission. What I didn't understand then was that the universe had tossed me a detour. I was heartbroken. None of this made any since. The book cloud was clear in the only letters that it ever showed me. I was dumbfounded and it showed.

I left abruptly from the counseling office without as much as an explanation, hearing Mr. Palmer's voice trail down the hallway. I didn't even make it to the front door. I headed to the back and fell onto the hammock in tears. I wept as if I had lost a loved one. Now, I would be forced to apply to USC whether I wanted to or not.

The book cloud lied to me or at the very least it mislead me. Why? I was furious. Anger took hold of me like a fierce storm on a mission. I stayed in my room. My temper was short with everyone. I cried so much that I was beginning to wonder if there was any water left inside of me.

I was a boat without a sail. A graduate without a home and a dream that suddenly felt like a nightmare. I was as miserable as a fly in a black widow's web. Even Josh noticed my onery attitude.

As I lay in my hammock looking at the stars and fighting back tears who were more stubborn then me as they glided down my cheeks, I felt a strong arm pull me into his bosom and just let me cry. For a long moment there was just silence, and Josh's cheek snuggled softly on my forehead.

"You wanna talk about it?" He said.

"I don't even know where to start." I said.

"You mean the woman who has words for everything, doesn't know where to start?" He laughed.

"Josh." I said laughing. "You can be so stupid at times." I laid back on his chest.

"Made you laugh, didn't I?" He replied.

"Yeah, you did." I said. "Remember when I told you about the book cloud?" I said.

Josh raised up and looked at me. "Yeah, weirdest story I ever heard. It still blows my mind at how the universe chose you."

I took a deep breath and raised my body up from Josh's bosom. "You and me both, freaks me out sometimes." In my eyes stood the memory and the scene of the cafeteria where the blue bench sat facing the sky. Like I was there again, I saw the book cloud and, I begin telling Josh about that day that change my life forever all over again.

"I had a serious urge to use the little girl's room, so I raised the paddle and took the key. For some reason, instead of going back the way I came, I took a left towards the cafeteria and there it was, a cloud in the sky shaped like an open book with four letters." I said. "I saw those letters in the book cloud that day and nothing else."

Josh shook his head and just like before his eyes still carried a mix of shock and a *what the hell?* I almost burst out laughing at his reaction, but my mixed up emotions were seriously fighting each other. Josh exhaled and cleared his throat and spoke.

"This story amazes me every time I hear it?" He said. "I still can't believe you waited so long to tell me."

"Josh, I was 13 at the time. I thought I was crazy when it just appeared to me so bold like that." I replied. "I didn't think you or anyone else would believe me. So, I just kept quiet."

"I guess it was a lot to hold." He looked at me. "I don't see how you did it. You have to know that I'm always here for you me."

"I do. I've always known that Josh. But we were young." I replied. "from the first day it revealed itself to me, I have been trying to figure out what it was trying to tell me." I said. "Some of it I still don't understand. And now with UCLA not having a major in journalism, I don't get it. I'm confused."

"Maybe it wasn't saying that you would grow up and attend UCLA. Maybe UCLA was for somebody else?" He said.

"Josh." I looked at him. "But what about the career center field trip in Mrs. Sal Lee's class. Remember that?" I said.

"Yeah, I remember you fleeing to the college corner and getting cozy on the couch flipping through a UCLA catalog."

"It wasn't like that." I said. "What made me go over there was that the catalog was just sitting there like somebody had planted it there for me. I swear." I said. "Why couldn't it have been any other catalog. Why UCLA?"

"I wished I could answer that, but I can't. So, are you saying that this book cloud confirmed you going to UCLA?" He said.

"I thought so then, but now I'm not so sure." I said.

"Why?" He said.

"Josh, are you listening to me." I said. "UCLA does not have a journalism major. Duh!"

"It's not meant to be then. Apply to USC. They've got the best journalism school in the country. You've got a syndicated column in the Gazette. I'm sure they already have a space for you." He said. "You would be crazy not to apply there."

"I don't want to go to USC." I pouted. "I wanna go to UCLA. The book cloud was clear. Those were the only four letters it showed me."

"Maybe it wasn't giving you UCLA for you Me. Have you ever thought that UCLA was a pathway to Olivia and Moose." He said. "Isn't that surgeon who performed Olivia's transplant from UCLA? And your editor from the Gazette an alum at UCLA. Maybe the tiny path behind the book cloud was the trail leading you to everything you have now? Would it be so bad if we were trojans instead of Bruins?"

"But I thought you were dead set on applying to UC Irvine. The beach cities, majoring in Urban Studies, and of course girls." I laughed.

"Me, LA has beach cities, and women," he whistled. "I'd major in art history if it meant you applying to USC will allow you to live your best life. You've got a dam good start to your future Me. You need to see it through."

I was speechless. My brain went numb. I leaped into Josh's arms and held him tight. I knew he loved me. Today proved how much.

Though I hadn't recognized it. God had ordained a detour in my life for a reason. Somehow, I had gotten it all wrong. What Josh had said made sense in a way. But stepping back in that moment, it didn't. What about the catalog at the college corner in the career center. UCLA in the book cloud, and Dr. Davis a graduate of UCLA. There were too many factors that were hard to ignore.

For years, I hadn't told anybody that secret, not even Josh. Now, I was confronted with a new truth. A truth that even I couldn't ignore. It seemed so simply then. The complexity of it was why me, and what did it all mean? Slowly, it was starting to reveal itself.

Grief is a funny thing. Experiencing it is like climbing Kilimanjaro without oxygen. In grief, you are so consumed that the loss itself takes total control over your entire being. Not being able to apply to UCLA was like a death in the family, and the universe sent Josh to help me rediscover my path and find my way back.

From the very beginning, I wanted answers. Answers that would only come from challenges and discovery. In the beginning, I just wanted to read the book and know it's story. What I didn't know was that I was the story and my story had yet to be written.

What I had not realized through my season of grief was UCLA was the gateway to my future, not the college I was supposed to attend. The hammock gave me solace and wisdom. The journal that Daddy had bought for me for graduation introduced me to a new passion I didn't know that I had. Writing became my voice and my contribution in which I would serve the world.

Through journaling, I was honing my craft as a writer and surrendering to the universe to which my gift was so graciously given. In Journaling, I discovered the power of writing. The influence that words could command by simply speaking from your soul and evoking truth. This became bigger than just writing down my thoughts but exploring how I could use these words to carry out a mission to do good.

Little did I know that as I attended Malcolm High School that I would meet a loudmouth jock by the name of Moose Gentry who thought it cute to pick on the smart kids for the sake of being an ass. The opposition that occurred between the two of us, and eventually Josh was carefully orchestrated by the universe for a greater purpose. Moose rattled something inside of me to stand up for the brainiacs, while God was working his plan to do a twofold, heal Olivia and her son.

In the strangest way, Moose's confession of Olivia's illness struck a cord with me, and I knew I had to do something. Olivia and I bonded in a way that today stills amazes me. Through Olivia, I learned to see Moose in a new light and as her condition deteriorated, I used my gift of words and composed a letter to a surgeon that I had seen maybe a two minute segment on 60 minutes to serve a woman who had become my friend.

My letter moved a doctor to do a heart transplant on a woman he would have never had the opportunity to meet and save if I would have never picked up my journal and discovered the power of the written word. My purpose was clear. If I wanted to make changes in this world, it would come through the influence of words.

Moose was my by-pass in discovering the gift inside of me that I needed to discover. Dr. Davis confided in me that he couldn't get the letter I had written out of his mind nor his heart. He was so impressed with it that he forwarded it to a friend of his at the Gazette, and my career as a writer had begun. Josh was right. UCLA was my path and it had lead me to every open door that was meant for me.

CHAPTER ELEVEN
FOLLOW ME

"And Jesus, walking by the sea of Galilee, saw two brethren, Simon called Peter, Andrew his brother, casting a net into the sea: for they were fishers. And he saith unto them, follow me and I will make you fishers of men. And they straightway left their nets and followed him." Matthew 4:18-20

A CALLING TO A HIGHER PURPOSE IS ALMOST ALWAYS DONE WHEN you least expect it. Usually it happens when your young, and sometimes it happens when you are seasoned and have had some difficulties, or tragedies take place in your life. You're never prepared for it. Almost always overwhelmed by it, and you question why you were the chosen one and pinpoint an individual or a group more equipped to perform the task then you.

The bible says in **1 Samuel 16:7** *"But the LORD said unto Samuel, look not on his countenance, or on the height of his stature; because I have refused him: for the LORD seeth not as man seeth; for man looketh on the outward appearance, but the LORD looketh on the heart."* The heart of a human being is his or her soul that shoulders compassion, empathy and coerces one to take on a task that may appear to be insurmountable. It forced David to take on Goliath. Dr. King to take on the bus boycott in

Alabama and become the father of the Civil Rights Movement. Moses to confront the Pharoh and eventually deliver God's people from the cruel bondage of slavery.

Credence is deep with God and it is how he measures the ability of the man or woman in generating transformation to the cause in which he requires change. Agents of change receive nudges, visions, and whispers that are meant strictly for them. Though they have no understanding of what it all means, what they do know is that whatever their jolt was, it was something they could not explain, and left them with way too many questions.

God loves questions. When we question things, he knows that we seek answers. In order to get the understanding we seek, we must bypass our flesh and get in tune with our spirit. Fleshly eyes could not have drawn Moses to a bush that burned but was not consumed. Nor could it have compelled David to fight a giant, or King to get involved in a movement that altered the course of history.

Like Moses, I too was amazed to see a cloud shaped in the form of an open book, looking directly at me like it had a message. It did, and in my questions, and my persistence in finding the answers, eventually it made sense as to why I was privy to see it in the first place. The fact that it appeared open really captured my attention, and I couldn't take my eyes off of it. I must have stared at it as much as it was gawking at me. At 13, I had many questions, inquiries that started me on an impeccable journey I will never forget.

I had never seen anything like it, and I wondered why it picked me to see it. I'm surprised that I even saw the small path behind the open book. In my deep gaze, my eyes had probably shifted a few centimeters up and there it was hidden behind the book that got my upmost attention. In that moment, it didn't register that the two were connected.

Somehow, I shifted my eyes back to the book and when I did it dropped the letters of UCLA. At this point the book had all my attention. For years, I kept what I had seen a secret. I never spoke a word to Josh my most trusted confidant, and I never even thought about mentioning it to my parents, or my two older sisters, Sett, and Zuri.

It's not that they would not have believed me. They would have. However, I didn't understand what I had saw. I hadn't a clue of how to explain it. Nor was I ready to see the look in my mother's eyes and see in them what I already knew.

After I saw it, I felt different. I felt as if the kid in me had died and the adult that stood silent inside, stepped into my soul and slowly slide into its rightful place. I begin to think differently. I yearned for more responsibilities, so I decided that I needed a job, and I got one at the Farmer's Market with Josh. I started analyzing things, questioning things, and through my journal that Daddy had bought me for a graduation present, I began to pick a part the image I had seen in the clouds that day piece by piece.

The hammock that Daddy had finally put out in our backyard became my burning bush. Through it, my expedition began. I could not have predicted crossing paths with Moose and being guided to Olivia. It was like God paused a moment in time and allowed Olivia's heart to get sick so that he could use me, the community, and the letter that I had written to get the attention of a pristine surgeon to create a miracle for Olivia. By it my purpose was defined. my future shaped by using my writing ability to speak and draw attention to those in need and to serve humanity.

Olivia and I became connected in ways that I could never have imagined. Olivia's heart was bigger than her illness. It was because of her that I began to see her son that I disliked differently. He started to see me differently too. He saw me go out of my way to help save a woman that I didn't even know. I was Compelled like Moses, David, and Dr. King to serve a purpose greater than myself, to have empathy for a guy I once loathed because Olivia could have been my mother, and if she had been I would have wanted Moose to do the same for me.

The flesh is never obligated to do anything, but the heart reaches deep. Cit swore that Moose fell for me because I helped save his mother. In her opinion, he had made up in his mind that no matter what I thought. No matter how much I resisted him that I was already his. He was handsome, persistent, kind, and so patient with me that my stubbornness was no match for his heart.

What I didn't know then that I know now is that God already had a plan to restore Olivia and in turn heal Moose. I believe that seeing UCLA in the book cloud was the path to the surgeon, Dr. Davis to perform Olivia's transplant surgery, and provide a nearby college for Moose to play football, staying close to his mom. For me, it was my gateway to a career I never knew existed inside of me, and a route in the form of a detour leading me to USC.

I stopped questioning why I was chosen. Stopped over thinking the details, and just learned to be open and embrace whatever circumstances that came. I came to understand that I didn't have all the answers, and I understand that I may never have them. What I know for sure is that before I was born, I was given a powerful gift to change situations, attract attention to causes that may never reach the resources they would need to reach in order to create change in situations they needed.

I know that words carry incredible power. The power to condemn, inspire, or change any situation, and alter the sequence of our history. What I didn't know was that the words in my letter to Dr. Davis influenced his decision to transform Olivia's condition. The letter outlined my purpose and altered my life forever. The road to Olivia was really a road to me. Olivia gave me a determination that gives me chills until this day. Beyond the tears that I shed for Olivia and Moose, somehow, I knew that if she died then I would die to. When I looked in her eyes, I saw life and it was that life inside of her that instructed me to fight for her with the only thing that I knew how, and that was with words.

My empathy for Olivia and Moose ran deep. I didn't know it then but as I composed the letter to Dr. Davis each word was like water hitting a rock. I made each word count and penetrated his heart like rainwater striking gravel.

Though I was not called like Peter to follow Jesus, I was summoned to follow him through an open book. I knew the moment that I saw it that something special would take place in my life. I didn't know when, or how, for the details were very sketchy. But something in my gut told me that because of what I had witnessed, my life would never be the same.

What I learned from this experience was that God calls you according to what interest you. At least that was the case for me. He knew that I would pay attention to an open book in the sky then anything else he may have chose to fling up there. He knew I was a reader and that nothing captured my attention like a great book. He knew by giving me scattered details that I would not hesitate to divulge into a search for answers which would direct me to my purpose.

The vision in the book cloud lit fire to my soul that all the water in the world could not put out. To discover who I was and to find my purpose in this life was to write my own story. Day by day. Page by page, I was piecing together clues, uncovering who I was and quietly finding my intention. They became my answers, the cause to serve a principle bigger than myself. Above it all was a greater renewal of the human spirit that I could never have imagined.

Olivia's new heart carried power. It transformed an entire community making them believe that anything was possible. Its arrow had purposely stung my heart and Mooses' and I was ill equipped to fight the love that jumped from it. The book had deliberately left out that detail, and it struck me as to why it believed that at such a young age, I needed that kind of love.

Moose had gotten his claws into me when I was just 14. At 15, we officially became the couple that we secretly were behind my father's back. Moose, my two older sisters, Mama, Olivia, Noah, and yes Josh had persuaded Daddy to break his rule of his daughters waiting until the magic age of 16 to date. Everybody was held responsible for me dating Moose so young. Moose even showed me the contract Daddy made him sign, insuring that I finish college and absolutely no sex at all even when I turned 18.

I was dumbfounded that Daddy would even do such a thing and stunned that Moose would be crazy enough to sign it. I took a deep breath and just stared at Moose. He hunched his shoulders and gave me a sheepish grin. I sighed and shook my head at him.

"Don't be like that." He said, wrapping his arms around my waist. "I love you." He placed his forehead next to mines then kissed me. "I would leap over a million moons just to be with you." He kissed me again, and again.

"I feel like he doesn't trust me." I said. "I bet Mama doesn't know anything about this bogus contract." I said, rolling my eyes and sighing. "Does she know?" I asked.

Mooses' eyes told the story long before his mouth did. "I…I suppose not, but I figure we can always edit the parts we don't like." He grinned and kissed me again. It was the kind of kiss that makes a girls toes curl and her Charlie's swell. Mooses' kisses were kryptonite. And Daddy's words were just words, and besides graduating from college, I was about to violate the part of the contract that would have made Daddy lose his mind.

At this point in my journey, Moose had no idea of my vision I had of the book cloud, nor the path in the clouds that led me to him and Olivia. I wanted to tell him, and I wondered why I hadn't. The right time would come and when it did, I would tell him. He needed to know the back story and how fate had plans for us long before we knew each other existed. Why the universe picked Moose for me and me for him is still a mystery to me.

In the beginning, we were so different. Moose was cocky and high strung. Me confident and low key. I had a heart. Moose had a stone. His attitude blinded his truth. But when I chased Josh and followed him down a row of cornfields where I thought he was hiding, destiny had me run into Moose and that's when his story unfolded.

A story is like a good fishing hole. The hook treads in the waters and scans the river for fish. Prior to catching the big fish, the fishhook may bring up algae, a toy, a bra, a couple of blankets coiled around each other disguising themselves as the big catch of the day. Moose was my catch divinely designed by the universe bypassing every boy I thought right for me.

The book withheld so much of my story. Probably because it knew I would try and change what I didn't like and rally around what I did. I would have botched USC and chose a school that was not in God's plan for me. The vision of the book cloud burned a fire so deep in my soul that it drove me in ways I couldn't believe. What I didn't know then, but I get now is that the reason the book cloud had no story, was because the narrative to be written was unfolding, and I had to be groomed to write it.

Word by word. Line by line. I was piecing together clues and discovering my role. There were questions that needed answers. And a cause to serve a bigger purpose so much bigger than me. Yes, Olivia needed a new heart, but so did Moose, whose stony heart was about to undergo a spiritual transformation.

In the "Grinch That Stole Christmas," the heart of the Grinch grew three sizes the day he changed. Mooses' heart dissolved from a rock to a caring soul when he saw a community rally around his mother and Dr. Davis perform her surgery. He was not the Moose that I had gotten introduced to that fall day as a freshman. As he changed, so had I. And in that moment enemies had become friends who fell in love.

God in his infinite wisdom had thrown out a hook in the sky that day. It was a perfect pitch that took anchor in my soul. I followed every current. Hit some rocks, resisted being caught and coming to surface because as humans do, I feared the unknown. Fear, I learned is part of your journey in following a path that lays out a naked road map with very little direction. Not knowing what will unfold once you get there, and somehow still mustering the courage to follow a path that's uncertain, is nothing but sheer bravery and unadulterated faith.

Follow what is good. Follow the deepest whispers of your soul that speak from a voice that your spirit will always understand. Listen to the inner GPS, that spiritual guidance that is always ready to help when you align yourself with the breaths of the universe. Learn to just pay attention and know that the universe will always have your back.

Moose was quite disappointed when he found out that I would be headed to his rival school, USC. At first, I was greatly disappointed to. I believe the book cloud when it revealed UCLA, and just assumed as only a 13 year old would that when I graduated from high school, I was going to UCLA. I held unto it so strong that when I found out that UCLA didn't have my major, I freaked, and I was mad at everybody until Josh talked to me.

To my surprise, I learned from my advisor that the work that I had put into the Gazette equaled out to two years of book work, and my two years at SC would be reduced to one year of course work and a year of field work in investigative journalism, and sports, my choices. I was besides myself and my parents through the roof. By nothing less then a godsend, Josh and I walked up on a two bedroom, and one and a half bath in Manhattan Beach. On a whim, we drove down to Manhattan Beach, and discovered this gem knowing from the onset that it belonged to us.

The husband of the couple that was supposed to rent out the apartment received a job offer overseas, and just like that it was on the market and Josh nor I hesitated to snatch it up. Moose, Josh, and some of Mooses' football buddies moved us in. By the first week of June Josh and I had settled comfortably into our new place. Mama nor Daddy was too found of us moving in nearly two months early. Surprisingly, neither was Nadine. However, Booker who seemed to be getting better was thrilled.

Josh and I had our reasons for moving down to Manhattan Beach two months before our semester started. We were following our hearts and a hunch that told us that we needed to get to know our new city. We needed to sink our toes in the sand of a new life that had its own road map. We needed to take hold of a new chapter that seemed like it was frozen in time and waited patiently for us to begin the trail.

On a trip down from our place in Forest Ranch, California to our new place, Daddy and I worked on dinner while Josh entertained Nadine, Mama, and Booker. Cutting up bell peppers, Daddy turned, stopped and looked at me. He was proud I could see it and he seemed to be amazed that I was all grown up and was about to enter college.

"Look at you." He completely stopped chopping vegetables. "I remember the day we brought you home from the hospital." He smiled. "So innocent and just days old. Now, you're all grown up." He smiled again.

"No matter how old you get." He said. "You will always be my little girl." He hugged me tight.

"Good." I said. "Cause, I wouldn't want it any other way." I kissed his cheek.

"Your Mama and me are mighty proud of you." He smiled, turning catfish.

"Thank you." I smiled, placing peppers, broccoli, carrots, and cauliflower in a saucepan with seasonings, and lightly browning them. "Daddy," I said, adding brown rice in the skillet. "Why in the world did you make a contract with Moose like that?"

"Because I want you to finish up at SC, and I've seen the way that boy looks at you." He said taking out some fish. "That boy's crazy about you and he's been asking me for your hand since you were 16, well 15, if I count the month before your birthday."

"What!" I said. "Josh had told me." But coming from my Daddy made me nearly lose my breath.

"What, he never told you?" Daddy said.

"No, Josh did. But it didn't really register until now." I said stirring the chicken stock. "I can only guess you said no."

"Of course, I did. You are gonna finish college first and continue to blossom in that career of yours." He smiled proud. "Now that you're 18, I know that boy will ask me again. He's persistent. I'll give him that."

"I'm sure you've scared him off by now." I said covering the rice.

"Who?" Daddy snickered and put more fish in the skillet. "That boy doesn't know how to be scared. Trust me, he'll ask again."

"You'll just say no again. He'll be asking until I'm 30." I said.

"That's the plan." Daddy said and laughed.

"Daddy," I said. "But I love him. I'm not saying he'll ask again. But if and when he does, I wish you'd say yes. You know I'll finish college, and you know that I could never marry him if you didn't give him your blessing." I said, wrapping my arms around him. "You will always be first in my heart." I said, kissing his cheek and laying my head in his bosom.

Daddy tilted his head downward to look at me, and he looked at me like I had lost my mind. I snickered at his reaction, but in my laughter, I meant every word I said. Daddy blessing Moose would be the consent I needed to know that Moose was as welcomed in Daddy's heart as I was. The look in Daddy's eyes had changed. He looked at me like the 30 year old he'd always joked about. It was as if she leaped out of my body and introduced herself to him for the first time. Whatever she had said to him he believed it and somehow when he looked at me again, it was different.

I caught Mama's eyes observing the moment. She looked as if her eyes had journeyed back to a past before I was born. A yesterday where I rested in her tummy waiting to enter the world. I could see my life through her eyes. Protruded belly. Swollen feet, back stiff and cranky.

When she blinked, I was born. A sip of sweet tea I was crawling. As she joined back in a conversation with Nadine and Booker, I was walking, running, and playing with Josh. A puff of her cigarette, I was in Junior high school. A toss of her hand at Nadine, and I was in high school. A look around our apartment and I had grown up and turned into the woman she had prayed for me to be. I could read her like she could read me and through her eyes I could see that Daddy was turning the page with me and following his heart.

CHAPTER TWELVE

EXPECTED END

"For I know the thoughts that I think toward you,
saith the lord, thoughts of peace, and not evil, to
give you an expected end. Jeremiah 29:11

THERE HASN'T BEEN A DAY THAT'S GONE BY THAT I HAVEN'T thought about the vision that I saw in the clouds that soggy day. For years it haunted me and drove me to discovery and a life a 13 year old could never have imagined. I looked for it everyday like I looked for a good book. But for years it hid itself and pulled and tugged me into the life it had planned for me.

The elders I grew up with always used to say that when God calls you for something special that he knocks at your window first to get your attention. I used to laugh when I heard them say it. But I am not laughing now. I remember that day like a fresh cup of coffee. The rain didn't just tap at my window, it knocked on it hard like it wanted to wake me and like it wanted to tell me something important.

I thought I was dreaming at first until I woke up. I remember that morning being a cold day. From my window I could see that the sky was covered with blackness, and I could see pools of water being dumped from the sky. From the way the day looked outside, I knew that Mama was not letting me go to school. Nonetheless, I washed my face, brushed my teeth, and showered anyway.

By the time I showered and ate breakfast, the rain had stopped. Josh cracked his bony knuckles against the door, then entered. He sat at the table briefly and grabbed some bacon left on the tray and made himself a sandwich. I don't know what made him do it, but he put his icy hands on my face, and I jumped. I smacked his thigh and through our horseplay our bus pulled up.

Mama was reluctant that morning in letting me go to school. From the shower, I could hear her and Nadine talking. I don't know how I could tell but somehow, I could feel her looking out of the window gawking at the pouring rain.

"It's raining waterfalls out there Nadine. I don't know about you girl, but if this rain doesn't let up, I'm not letting my baby go to school today." Mama inquired.

"Girl," Nadine said. "You preaching to the choir."

It did let up and before Mama could shove her reluctancy on me, I was out of the door eating what was left of my bacon sandwich. For the rest of the day, it didn't drop a bead of water. By the time I had got comfortable in social studies class, I felt the warmth of the sun on my arms, and it felt like a warm hug on a freezing October day. I don't know if it was the apple juice, or the water I had during break before going to social studies class. Whichever one it was, or both combined, I had to pee like something awful. That's where the whole thing began.

God woke me up out of my sleep by balling up his mighty fist thumping my pane as if it was an emergency. It was. I just didn't know any of the details at the time. As Olivia began recovering from her surgery, she shared a testimony with me that gives me goosebumps until this day. Her health had been failing for months. A walk to the kitchen was draining.

After a series of test, the unthinkable was revealed. Olivia needed a new heart and had been put on the transplant list October 20, 1995, the same day God knocked on my window and later that day anointed me with the vision. I remember weeping profusely like I had lost a loved one. And I cried even more at God's urgency in smacking my window. Suddenly his timing made so much since. Throughout my young life, all I heard from my elders was about God's timing. *"He may not come when you want him, but he always comes on time."*

It didn't mean much to me then. I was a teen riding bikes with Josh, secretly reading Zuri's diary about her boyfriend Brandon, reading every classic I could get my hands on, and of course fantasizing about being Picasso Brown's girl. Life was easy and simple for me then. Little did I know that I was about to undergo a massive transformation.

Olivia didn't understand my wailing at first. I think she thought I had gotten overwhelmed by the story she was sharing with me. It was bigger than that. You see, God could have chosen anyone that he wanted for the task. A more seasoned adult who would have been more equipped to handle the situation at hand. I was a child tossed into an adult role with no experience in dealing with a woman with a dying heart who urgently needed a transplant. To this day, I have no idea of why he chose me?

Olivia consoled me in her arms and assured me that she was fine. In fact, she swore that she had never felt greater, and that the energy that she had was a strength that came directly from God. As I cried, Olivia cried, and then I told her what happened to me on that rainy October day and how the vision eventually led me to her and Moose. Her face displayed complete shock. Her lips trembled, and like a ravishing waterfall, tears sprung from her eyes uncontrollably. She understood my tears, and she got why I was crying.

I knew I had to tell my parents about the vision before Olivia did. I also needed to get to Moose before she got to him. I didn't want to have to answer a zillion question from him. First things first, I had to tell my parents. I think I had a secret pack with myself not to tell what I had saw to anyone. Then, out of the blue here came Josh, and I felt compelled to tell him my secret.

I had no idea that Olivia would share that portion of her life with me. In fact, for the many interviews I had done with her, surprisingly it never came up. Her story captured an audience for me that I could never have predicted. Since she shared this component, I felt like an important element of her story was missing. I had received many letters from my loyal readers for a follow-up. Now, I think I had something to share with them.

I hadn't planned how I would tell my parents. That's because I never thought I'd be put in the position of having to tell them. I was learning that timing was everything. Time and the universe had spoken loud and clear. I stopped working on my outline and took a long exhale. I left my room and entered the kitchen. Mama and Daddy both turned around and looked at me and smiled.

I scooped up some of Daddy's dirty rice and grabbed a piece of Mama's roast chicken still trying to figure out how to break it to them. Before I could figure out how I was going to tell them, Mama took one look at me and said. "What's on your heart baby girl?"

I stopped eating dirty rice and just looked at her for a minute. "How do you always know?"

"Because I know my daughter," she touched my nose. "It's been brewing in you for a while." She said. "The good lord anointed you to help Olivia. That much I know." She smiled and took fresh bread out of the oven. "Now, what do you want to add to that?"

I almost dropped my chicken. Thank God that Daddy had quick hands. He laughed as our eyes met. "Baby Cakes you alright?" He just looked at me.

"Yeah." I said looking at Daddy. "Mama just spooks me sometimes." I replied as I swallowed hard. "I don't remember saying anything about it." I said, looking like a deer in headlights.

"You didn't have to." She dipped her basting brush in hot butter and gently stroked the bread. "I saw a change in you that summer you graduated from Junior high school."

I nearly choked on the rice, and my eyes bulged out like I was scared. In a sense, I was. Now, I had to figure out how to tell them what Mama seemed to already know.

"What?" She placed a small piece bread on my plate. "You want to tell me something?"

"I thought I did. But now I don't even know how to say it." I said.

"Every story has a beginning Baby Cakes." Daddy said. "Just say it."

I took a deep breath then blurted it out. "I had a vision of an open book and a small path in the clouds when I was 13 years old on the same day Olivia got her diagnosis of needing a new heart." I said out of breath as if I had just ran the 50 yard dash. "That morning, raindrops were thumping on my windowpane like it was trying to wake me up, and like it had something urgent to tell me."

Mama dropped her basting brush on the floor, and her eyes widened. Daddy's mouth opened wide and stayed opened for a minute or so. His eyes registered shock. I could see that day in both of their eyes like both of them had some vague regulation of what they were doing in that moment.

There was a peculiar silence standing bold in the kitchen. Cooking was put on a brief hold. Mama placed her hand over her mouth and suddenly her eyes flooded with tears. She opened her arms and I found myself in them.

Daddy wrapped his arms around the both of us and pulled both of us into him. For a moment, not a word was spoken. Right there in that moment it felt like I was getting a big hug from God. Mama just cried like I never seen. It was a grateful cry and a cry like she was thanking God that he allowed me to slip from under her protective grasp.

"You know I almost kept you home that day." She said wiping tears from her cheeks. "Oh, thank God, he pushed you out of the door that day." She wiped more tears from her face with the bottom half of her apron.

Daddy took a deep breath and rubbed Mama's back. "Little did we know that what appeared as the worse day of her life, God had it covered through our little girl." He hugged me.

"I'm sorry I didn't tell you back then." I said. "But I didn't know how."

"Baby." Daddy looked at me. "You were 13, at the time. I can only imagined what was going through your mind then." He said. "It's okay. Just know that you can always come to us with anything." He replied. "We're always here for you, you know that." He kissed my cheek.

I knew that to be true more than I ever did. Over Daddy's shoulder, I could see the hammock that had given me and Josh so much comfort. Without thinking I headed out of the back door and landed in it. I took a deep breath and just stared at the deep blue sky. A breeze tickled my face as I lay there in my hammock suddenly thinking about my life. I don't remember having a plan for my life at 13. But if I did, God laughed, scratched it out, and wrote me a new one.

I seemed to have skipped over my teen years and leaped right into adulthood with no sort of training. There seemed to be this force that provided directions and placed people in my path like Dr. Davis and the passion in my heart that guided me to pour out my soul to him in a letter. I didn't have time to breathe, think, or be scared. A life was being hijacked and I reacted in the only way that I knew was with a pen, then finalizing my words on my laptop.

I didn't expect him to answer, and I certainly didn't expect for him to do the surgery, but he did. Before Olivia went under the knife, I knew she would not just live to fight another day. I knew that she would soar. I never expected the life I was given. I didn't expect to be the one he used to get Olivia to Dr. Davis, but I was. What I didn't understand then that I have come to know now is that God covered me with goodness, protected me from evil and brought me into a great life that I never would have anticipated.

From the moment I was born, to the moment I had seen the vision that October day, before I could figure out what the heck was going on, I had already won. I took another deep breath and watched the leaves sway in the wind. I had looked for the open book in cloud for years. I thought that it might have more clues to offer. I thought it might give me a reason why it had showed up for only me to see it. I guess, I thought a lot of things. I never saw it again. But I didn't need to. It had took a special seat in my soul and waited for this day to come where seeing the vision and following my path was enough.

Every time I saw Olivia, I saw God. In her, I saw miracle healing power. I saw the dry bones and flesh covering bleached bones and through the breath of God I could see how he had breathed life into a dead soul. Like the disciples, onlookers, and his family who were clueless about Lazarus fate, so was I green about Olivia's illness, and how her life hung in the balance.

In the bible, Jesus purposely stayed away from where Lazarus body had been laid for four days. Jesus could have easily went to attend to him before he died. But he didn't. He needed to show the world that nothing is ever out of his reach, not even death. Even when you've been buried for four days, and your body begins to stink.

Timing is everything with God and he knows when to step in. With Lazarus it was four days. With Olivia, it was a year. I had to unravel the mystery. I had to discover the power of words and my connection with them and the ability to get the attention of those who read them. I had to meet Moose and have a confrontation with him. And I had to meet him one more time at Seth's Farm chasing Josh through cornfields, running directly into Moose again only to hear his story.

Somehow, he was different this time and so was his story. He wasn't picking on smart kids this time. He was scared to death of losing his mother whose heart was getting worse by the day. God had to put so many variables in place. He had to pull the stopple on the rain that day, or I wouldn't have been able to go to school. I had to run into Moose at

Seth's Farm that day and hear his soul. I had to see that last two minute segment on 60 minutes about Dr. Davis and all the successful, risky heart transplants he had done, or Olivia would have died.

Olivia was my Lazarus. Her sickness did not end in death and was deliberately planned so that the glory of God could once again be revealed. I never saw it coming. I was blindsided by all the challenges, twist, turns, and the obstacles, that I almost missed the miracle of perfect love.

No matter what you are up against. How difficult the hour. How long you stand at your red sea. Or how much it looks like your dream is about to die and your miracle took a detour. ***Gods got you, and you've already won.*** The bibles says in Jeremiah 1:5, ***"Before I formed thee in the belly, I knew thee; and before thou camest forth out of the womb I sanctified thee…"***

Our stories are already written. Our battles already won. The victories most sure, and our life plan mapped out to the most finite detail long before we are born. Rest assured that you are a part of God's thoughts, his plans, and for you there is an expected end.

CHAPTER THIRTEEN

THERE IS A SEASON

*To everything there is a season and a time for every
purpose under the heavens. Ecclesiastes 3:1*

THERE ARE NO ACCIDENTS, NO COINCIDENCES, AND NO SURPRISES to God. That surprising health issue, sudden job loss and that unplanned pregnancy may be a shock to you, but it doesn't catch God off guard. Everything has a season, a time, and every incident that happens in our lives has a purpose.

Whatever your assignment is it is assigned to you before you were even created. No one else can have it, nor can the enemy stop it. There will be challenges, resistance, and detours. When your due season approaches, all hell will break loose.

The enemy will come at you so fierce that you will want to give up. Your flesh will tell you; you can't do it. That there's no way you can climb the next inch of your mountain and claim your blessing because it's not meant for you to have it. After all your hard work, after all your tears, prayers, worry, and sleepless nights, the devil will have you thinking that God is shuffling back on his promise. Well, the devil is a lie. No matter what the enemy does. No matter what he uses to try and stop what God has ordained for you, rest assured that God always delivers on his promises. We all have a time.

A season from birth to discover who we are and why we showed up on this planet in the first place. Eventually your path will make its presence known and ready or not the assignment you've been given will show up.

Moose showed up way before Olivia did and I never even noticed it. Moose was the type of blessing that showed up ugly, disguised as a hot mess that took me by storm and caught me off guard. In the beginning, I hated him. He came across as an arrogant bully with a "I can do whatever I want" attached to his resume. Being who I was, I was not having it, and I reacted.

We were as opposite as fire and water. He had to have an entourage. He needed to be the center of attention even if it meant being loud and obnoxious, picking on the brainiacs to get laughs and be crowned intimidator of the yard. Though I was a freshman, I was unaccustomed to following rules by juniors and seniors who were as mature as a toddler in a toy store. My sister Sett amongst others were the exception to the rule.

It was not like I was given a guidebook on how to handle the Mooses' of the world in high school. Nor was I given a road map that guided the cool kids to a hidden pocket on campus away from the pretenders who wore mask to hide their identity. Like every freshman, I had to find my way and carve out my own space away from the madness. I yearned for a spot on campus where all of us kids who were different, artsy, brainiacs and vibers could be accepted. I looked for a place where smiles bloomed every day, inspiring others was as constant as breathing the air, and helping a neighbor, or a teacher afterschool, was as cool as drinking a coke on a blistering day.

I don't think that I ever found that place on campus. What I discovered was that they were pinches of places like that at our high school everywhere. Us vibers as we called ourselves, eventually discovered that in life vibers didn't just have a segregated space they could call their own. Positive vibes were everywhere in the world, and at such a young age, we were just finding our places.

I wish that I could say that at these hot spots Moose didn't appear at times. It wasn't often, but when he or his peeps drifted by any of our spots, it was strange considering that he wasn't a viber. I don't know why I paid it any attention at all. I don't know why I was always the one who would see him and nobody else would including Josh.

Most of the time we were too busy vibing, talking about who need help. What senior's yards needed raking? Who was going to walk Eddie Beaumont to the market to help him in case he had a seizure? To the Mooses' of the world, I'm sure we were just a bunch of flakes with way too much time on our hands. But despite the gossip, we were proud of who we were and in joy of doing good amongst the chatter.

Josh and I seemed to be settling into who we wanted to become. We knew that being freshmen was like digging our way out of a dark hole. We didn't want to wait for the upper classman to adopt us in their circle, then conjure up stupid stuff for us to do so we felt like we were fitting in. So, we created our own identity, and forced the hand of respect.

Sett and Ruth had eased into the vibe. Not that they were ever against it, it was there way of allowing us to make our way up the ladder. Out of nowhere, they wore matching vibe t-shirts that read: *"Feel the Vibe."* As they passed Josh and I and the other vibers in the hallway, they tossed us the peace sign making their way down the corridor.

Further down the hall was Moose and at the time his clinging vine Jazmine and the other silly's who followed him like a rockstar. He and his goofballs sickened me every time I saw them. My vibe would immediately be put on hold when he crossed my path. I remembered this one moment like I recall a good book.

Josh and I were headed home from school through the front entrance and Moose was entering the doors going the opposite direction. Of course his vine was with him, sticking to him like a stamp to a letter. For no unknown reason, he just stopped at the door and eyeballed me like I was a main dish he wanted to try. It shook me to the point where the hairs on my arms stood at attention like soldiers.

It was the darndest thing that I'd ever seen. Moose was not found of me, nor I him. Since our altercation we didn't speak a word. We didn't even grace each other with a hi. The vine pulled on his arm like she was yanking fruit from a tree. When her tugging didn't suffice, she stood in front of him, and peered in his eyes. But his focus was elsewhere.

He gently pushed her aside and turned his athletic body towards me and just stared at me. He winked at me and then smiled. If Josh wouldn't have caught me, I would have slipped and broke something valuable. Josh looked at me like he always did when I did things that didn't make any sense to him. He looked at me like I was losing my marbles for something that made absolutely no sense.

He was a guy, and he didn't get it, nor would I expect him to. It was just weird, too weird. His strangeness had me reacting in a way that made Josh think that I was crazy. But that was just it, I wasn't crazy.

I couldn't digest the timing nor his reaction, his look, or his wink. It bothered me for the rest of the day. And as if that wasn't enough, timing had struck again when I bumped into Moose chasing Josh in Seth's cornfields.

I'm sure God had a big laugh. In fact, I could almost hear it. Soothing, yet thunderous, looking straight down on me shaking his head with the biggest smile, placing his free arm around time. When I think about what all took place for Olivia's miracle to happen, I get goosebumps about God's intricate plan.

I had to be born. Moose had to be born. We both had to grow to the point where God could use us. I had to meet Moose in a way that made me loathe him. I had to see that there was more to Moose than his false bravado that he was showing. I had to learn that enemies could and would become friends because there was a greater purpose involved.

I thought that Moose was so much different than me. He was to a certain degree. Through anger, and unadulterated stubbornness, I missed his will through his wink that day. Life is not about co-mingling, or vibing with folks who may have the same heart as you. It is more about feeling people who carry the emotion that they could never vibe with you.

That's why God stopped me dead center in the cornfields that day. Sometimes a wink, or a nod may be all you will get from a potential viber who yearns for change. Be open so that you don't miss it. One way or the other, God's plan for you will catch up with his purpose for your life.

Moose did have a heart. But what hid it and turned it was his mother's illness, and the dreadful fact that she might die. His story gave me a new vibe. It guided me to my purpose exactly the way God had planned. All of it led me back to the tiny path I saw in the clouds that day along with the open book. Now, it was all making sense.

In a nano second, us vibers switched from raking yards to organizing chores to help ease the load off Moose and his family's shoulders. We did everything from cleaning Olivia's kitchen to cooking meals, and bible study. Olivia was never alone and always loved up to point that even her dying heart absorb the care that was shown to her. Somewhere out there all that love was captured and the universe in its infinite timing, graced with mercy made a deal with a kind soul and that was it. Even the letter I wrote to Dr. Davis on Olivia's behalf was scheduled long before I was planned.

This new Moose made me as nervous as a cat surrounded by a bunch of street dogs with an agenda. I was uncomfortable with how he looked at me because it carried the look of love, and it was awkward. I thought it would stop after a while, but it didn't. It grew more intense and suddenly he had fell hard for me. When he did, everybody knew except for me.

Mooses' new heart had made him a piranha in love, and he had no problem in letting me know how he felt. I saw him everywhere at school. His eyes were always on me, and when they weren't I felt them. I discovered that under Mooses' stone was a heart the size of the Mississippi.

It was evident as I spent time at his house doing chores and getting to know a different side of him that I didn't know. He was a silent viber who needed healing and love. I would come to learn later that this is where I came in.

At school he was different and so where his friends who hung with him except the vine. Though she still tried to cling, he had cut her branches massively and her roots died. I would catch him gazing at me in ways that made me cringe. His gawking was personal. His eyes dripping with the "L" word that made my breathing labored.

At the age of 14, I was no match for what had been timed, orchestrated, and ordained by the giver of light. I caved eventually under his kindness, patience, and his potent kisses and the will of the universe. I never looked back. Moose proposed to me in front of our families on Christmas eve. If Josh wouldn't have caught me, I swear I would have fainted.

Moose placed my hand in his and looked at me, smiled, then kissed me and looked directly at Daddy. Daddy exhaled and shook his head slightly.

"Mr. Betts." Moose said. "We've been here before, and I've been turned down every time I've asked." He looked at me and kept going. "I love your daughter so much. I promise you and Mrs. Betts that I will take very good care of her. I am asking for your permission and your blessing to marry this beautiful woman so that I can finally make her my wife."

My eyes connected to Daddy's and there wasn't a word spoken between us. What I saw in his eyes first was that he had grown tired of Mooses' repetitive asking of my hand in marriage. He knew that he wouldn't stop until he got the answer that he wanted. Finally, I saw in his eyes, that I was ready. No, I hadn't finished SC, I was just a year into my college life, but I had a career and in my brief 18 years, I had lived.

Daddy wasn't looking at what I had left. He was looking at what I had done. What Moose was asking was totally against what he had hoped for. But he could trust me now and know that no matter what, I would graduate and make him and Mama proud. Olivia was already crying. Mama, Nadine, Sett, and Zuri joining her. As she wiped her eyes, she was egging Moose on as if there was something urgent that he needed to say but wasn't saying it fast enough.

"Mom! Okay, already." He said and laughed.

I was glad to see him have that moment with Olivia because I know that there were times, he thought he wouldn't. It made me nearly cry at the thought of it. She was so close to traveling to the other side, but God said different.

"Mr. and Mrs. Betts, especially Mr. Betts. I want you to know that I just signed a five year multi-million dollar deal with the Los Angeles Rams. So, can I please marry your daughter."

"Yes son." Daddy said. "Congratulations by the way. Now, I can rest from you asking me to marry my daughter." He giggled.

Moose screamed loud like he had sacked a quarterback, and then he lifted me in his arms and kissed me. "You hear that baby." Tears stood in his hazel eyes. "You hear that." He said. "Yes! So," Moose turned, dropped to one knee, and looked at me. "Baby, will you marry me?"

"Yes." I said. "Yes, I love you." I replied, then we kissed.

I had never seen a diamond that big. It looked like it practically took up my entire hand and I couldn't take my eyes off it. For a moment, time stopped and honored us. Mama took hold of my ring hand and smiled proud with tears running down her cheeks.

I took to her arms, unable to stop my own tears from falling. She wrapped her arms around me and held me tight. I felt her tears on my cheek. She felt mines on hers. I held on to her as tight as I could because I knew that this moment would never come again.

The hug that I received from my mother that day was the sort of hug that happens when there's a right of passage. When a girl passes from kid to womanhood, and her mother let's her go into the world to make her own way, to be wife and mother, it is a special moment that comes only once in a lifetime, and I wasn't about to miss it. When she did release me, there was Josh who whistled at my engagement ring and bragged about who had really picked it. I'm sure it came down to a debate between the two of them, then a compromised ensued. The result of their compromise was that I loved the ring, and my reaction showed it.

He kissed my forehead as he held my hands. "I got you." He said. "I got you." He turned his head slightly looking at Moose who was surrounded by both of our families with the biggest grin on his handsome face. "That's a good dude over there. He'll do right by you." He hugged me again and I laid in his arms embracing the moment.

I had seen the light at the age of 13, when it seeped through the sky to display the vision that would change my life forever. I had no way of knowing it then. I would have an illness that didn't belong to me dumped on me with not a clue of what to do at first. But that's where you learn who you are. In that period of "not knowing," in that moment of why me, in that hole of fear is where the "you" that God knows comes out.

We have no idea of what is to befall us when we arrive here. There is so much we have to learn about ourselves first then our families, and this world. Somewhere in this voyage, life opens up and the test begins. When it shows up, how it shows up, at what age it shows up is of no concern to us, or at least it shouldn't be. From zero to hero, it will all work out when you finally figure out that what's been driving you crazy has already been settled.

God chooses anyone, anywhere, any age, and at any time. He hunts for the ordinary, the scrooge, and the inexperienced like me. He provides what you need when you need it, and he knows when to lift you up and pull you out. You don't need to know all the answers. You don't have to try and be brave when you are really afraid. You just have to breathe and know that you're standing in the palm of the creator's hands and that he's got you.

Moose was my desert in the beginning and Olivia became my oasis. I could always tell when she was around by the sent of her Red Door perfume. That Christmas Eve that Moose proposed to me was no different. I smelt her before I felt the gentle arm around my shoulder. As she pulled me into her arms, I felt her heart thumping lively inside of her chest and it made me reflect on how our story had begun.

Over the years, I had come to understand the narrative as the universe unveiled it to me. Olivia was my path. Her heart was the open door to the life that was given to me. I needed her as much as she needed me.

Moose needed what football couldn't give him and I got that until he was factored into the purpose of the vision, then it didn't make sense. For the life of me, I couldn't understand why the universe allowed love to bloom in two people who were too young to understand love, its foundation, and the powerful affect it has on anyone it gets its claws into. I didn't know myself at 14, and Moose wasn't even close to knowing who he was at 17, or who he would become.

But when Olivia kissed my cheek and planted her green eyes inside of mines and said, "Thank you for saving my son." I got it. Moose needed love and the love that he needed could only come from me. His dedication, perseverance, and sweetness were so much bigger than him. He was as much a part of my path as Olivia was. Olivia needed a human heart, and he needed a spiritual one.

Love had chosen me before I was born. When it handed out my assignment, it handed me an incredible one. The final piece of the puzzle that had at times kept me up late at night, was finally revealed to me. It felt like a boulder was lifted off my shoulders, like I could freely breathe again. I didn't have to wonder why? And I didn't have any more questions. That's when I knew, and that's when you will know that, **"You've Already Won."**

THE END